The Quest for Self-Forgiveness:
Discovering the Secret
of Guilt-Free Living

Brilliant Redeemer
— BOOK ONE —

THE *Quest*
FOR SELF-FORGIVENESS

DISCOVERING THE SECRET
OF GUILT-FREE LIVING

Lynn Hare

FOREWORD BY JOHN ANDERSON

Many are the plans in a man's heart,
but it is the Lord's purpose that prevails.
(Proverbs 19:21)

To Ben
This story wouldn't be possible without your
love and grace.

To Sarah
I don't know you, but the Holy Spirit does.
He wrote this for you.

To Co-Co
Comforter and Counselor.

And to Tim
Whose quiet acceptance is my safe place, too.

Acknowledgments

Holy Spirit, I love You! You're my brilliant Redeemer.

Tim, thank you for cheering me on and extending patience, love, and practical help throughout the process of bringing this book from storyboard to completion. You're my best friend and champion!

Ben, your creativity and humor have been tremendous on our journey. Andy, what a joyful presence you have been in our home. Emily, I'm grateful for your help editing, praying through massive warfare, and teaching me kindness with your gentle spirit. Jill, you're a jewel.

Dad and Mom, I'm thankful for your generosity, prayers, and encouragement. Dad, I treasure the wonderful talks about our memories and how we've both grown through the years. Mom, the stories, songs, love, and faith you have poured into me have shaped my life and heart, too.

Maggie Terrell, exceptional coach and friend—I'm deeply amazed by your encouragement and ongoing support. With our God, we scaled a wall! Together, we've overcome the terrier barrier.

Dr. Bruce Cook and John Anderson, I'm deeply grateful for your discipleship and the gift of new spiritual altitudes. James Autry, thank you for showing me how to release Kingdom time, talent, and treasure through eternity with the intimacy, authority, and resources of Christ. Your apostleship has opened my eyes to runways in the supernatural. *Shalom!*

Ruth Lum, your prayers, joyous laughter and friendship have uplifted me to soar beside you. Alexis Alexander, I can't count how many times you have reached out to me with the rumbling sounds of heaven and reminders that we're shifting atmospheres as we look beyond what we can see. You both have provided perfectly-timed words that gave me the tenacity and courage to move forward.

Mentors Wendy Dunn, who taught me the meaning of Co-Co love, Kathie Nelson, Sue Miholer, and publishing guru David Sanford, I'm grateful for your godly wisdom.

Special thanks to the unseen warriors of powerful and effective intercession behind the story. Susan Ward, sister and friend, your sincere, steady prayers and timely words have carried me and encouraged my heart! Tami Estopare, Anna Chacon Funke, Cathy Rogers, Charles and Laura Harrel, Alison Wood, Dale Lawrence, Dr. Gayle Rogers, Lindy Swanson, Marilyn Rhoads, Kathy Ruckman, Gary and Nancy Lovelace, Erin Shepherd-Ham, Lucienne Sawyer, Sue Abrahamson, Trevor, Vicki, Nash and Brock Norris, and Stephanie Magno, your friendship and prayers have tangibly fortified me.

Kate Brady, you have personally empowered me with peace that dances, joy that rests, surges of optimism, and reminders to this Tuba that we are God's instruments.

Thank you, Tom and Bonnie Kopp, for releasing a passion for the nations—and the vision to impact leaders with Christ's profound forgiveness and love. You are heaven-sent role models whose missions work has been a delightful invitation to enter into His global move.

Thank you Nadine Dody, Dr. Charles and Laura Harrel, Elizabeth Dyan, Sherri Langton, Carrie Re, Joanna Echols, John Avery, Kathy Recchiuti, Mark Hiatt, Dr. Bob Allen, Meredyth Crofton, James and Hanna Humberd, Kevin and Lisa Jennings, Rich and Stacie Butler, and Mark and Sylvia Rogers.

I'm grateful for your friendship and love, Greg and Bonnie Knopf, who breathed and sang into my spirit the inspiration for writing, and Joe and Susy Saint, who also stir my soul with Holy Spirit love, compassion, and fire.

Pamela Cangioli, Kimberley Jace, Lisa Thompson, Alison Wood, Sue Miholer, and Susan Maas, thank you for your editing input on this project. What enormous contributions you've made. Nicole Miller, what exquisite cover design! And Christina Tarabochia and Tim Hare, fabulous job with internal formatting. You've all knocked one out of the park. No. Wait. To the moon.

It is not possible to list here all who have contributed to this project. Your faith, trust, and sincere investment in its message made this book possible. You mean the world and inexorable possibilities to me and every life this pebble in the pond touches with echoes of ever-widening ripples.

Endorsements

Lynn Hare has written a candid, courageous, and compelling account of her journey to self-forgiveness which will inspire and bring hope and healing to many others trapped in the vicious cycles of shame, guilt, blame, low self-esteem, self-hatred, self-sabotage, unforgiveness, isolation, depression, confusion, and/or unrighteous anger. *The Quest for Self-Forgiveness* provides practical steps to freedom and a way of escape from these self-destructive cycles and patterns of thought and behavior, and shows its readers the way forward to recovery, wholeness, and structural integrity and integration between body, soul and spirit. She intermingles compassion and colorful stories from her own life to provide helpful examples of God working in our midst and in our mess. Lynn's life now is a powerful message.

Dr. Bruce Cook
Chairman/CEO
Kingdom Congressional International Alliance (KCIA)
www.kcialliance.org
VentureAdvisers.com, Inc., www.ventureadvisers.com
Author of *Partnering With the Prophetic* and *Aligning With the Apostolic*

With brilliantly written and clever anecdotes that relate a powerful sequence of events and masterfully crafted creative words and phrases, Lynn Hare takes the reader on a spiritual adventure with God that leads to self-forgiveness. This story of Lynn's personal journey over the course of more than two decades will lead you to discover truths about self-forgiveness and come to peace with yourself.

In *The Quest for Self-Forgiveness*, you will discover what holds most people back from breakthrough in the area of self-forgiveness: their inability to appropriate God's grace for themselves. The Holy Spirit will be your guide on this journey of freedom—highly recommended and desperately needed in our unforgiving culture.

Dr. James Brewton
Founder and Senior Pastor
Community Empowerment Ministries, Inc.
Author of *From Footmen to Horsemen: The Rise of Commissioned, Kingdom Level Leaders* and *Back Porch Meditations: Holy Spirit Revelations"*
www.community-empowerment-ministries.org

This is by far one of the most practical, inspiring self-help books I've read in a very long time. Growing up in a world of self-perfectionism, self-recrimination, and often believable, yet deceitful lies from the enemy, Lynn managed, through the sheer grace of God's goodness, to mature into a woman who recognizes the key elements to peace, fulfillment, and wholeness. She found truth cloaked in a sea of love of God, love of self, and love of people, encapsulated in utter and total forgiveness—of self and others.

Lynn doesn't write simply about the significance of self-forgiveness, but provides her readers with very definitive and practical steps. Lynn takes you on a healing journey of working/walking out wholeness by using her own life's experiences. It simply can't get any better than that.

This is a practical handbook to self-healing and deliverance for those struggling with childhood memories, hurts, wounds, and long-lasting scars from traumatic and emotional episodes that have kept them bound throughout their adult life. This practical guide will catapult people into their destiny.

Dr. Gayle Rogers
President/Founder
Apostolic Coaching for Empowerment & Forever Free
Author of *The Whole Soul* and *Healing the Traumatized Soul*
www.doctorgayle.com

Lynn Hare has a pure heart for God and the things of God. In *The Quest for Self-Forgiveness* she will walk you through the most important journey of your life—how to forgive yourself. This is a timely book for the state of the world today, a must-read.

Ambassador Dr. Clyde Rivers
Honorary Ambassador at Large for the Republic of Burundi Africa
Golden Rule World Peace Ambassador Representative to the U.N.—New York for the Interfaith Peace-Building Initiative
President, I Change Nations
www.ichangenations.org

Aldersgate Conference Center, 2011. I was teaching a coaching class at the Oregon Christian Writers Summer Coaching Conference on a subject I've since forgotten. But I'll never forget one writer who sat near the back: eyes wide with wonder, a smile like sunshine. Furiously scribbling notes, she leaned forward in her seat as if my every word pumped breath into her.

That writer was Lynn Hare.

While I taught, Lynn's sheer delight in learning caught my eye. Then I read her writing—a gripping story about a car accident in which she and her baby boy sustained serious injuries. But those didn't match the emotional damage in Lynn: Her one second of inattention behind the wheel had caused the accident. A twenty-year battle with self-forgiveness began.

Our publication posted the story. Now it serves as the premise of Lynn's book *The Quest for Self-Forgiveness*. The same fresh writing is here as I saw in 2011 and an instant connection with readers. At some time in our lives, we've done the unthinkable to someone or to ourselves. Does God forgive us? Of course. Can we forgive ourselves? Well, that's tougher.

If you're one of those in the struggle, embrace your journey to forgiveness with God, guided by a woman who's been there. You won't regret the trip!

Sherri Langton
Associate Editor
Bible Advocate   www.baonline.org
Now What?   www.nowwhat.cog7.org

Forgiving others for their trespasses can be hard. Forgiving ourselves when our actions have hurt others is even harder. Lynn Hare knows firsthand what it's like when the tape of that long-past incident continues to replay in your memory over and over again. With each replay, the pain echoes through your mind. "If only I hadn't . . ." becomes your life's motto. Thankfully, Lynn has learned the lessons of self-forgiveness and passes along her insight to all who wrestle with the guilt from past actions or words. For such, *The Quest for Self*-Forgiveness is must-reading.

Nick Harrison
Author of *Power in the Promises* and
Magnificent Prayer

When one struggles to break out of a prison as Lynn Hare has, they can describe every brick and bar in great detail . . . and also the way of escape! Lynn has done an excellent job of explaining the many facets of freedom through forgiveness, including self-forgiveness. Her insights, biblical truths and prayers are powerful and anointed.

Pastor Nathan Daniel
Freedom Through Forgiveness Ministries
www.freedomthroughforgivenessministries.com
Author of *Freedom Through Forgiveness*

I wish you could join me for coffee or lunch with the author of this heartfelt, moving book. Lynn is honest about who she is, what she has done, and how deeply she has suffered and struggled. As well, Lynn is refreshingly, exuberantly in love with the Lord, her family, and life. This book beautifully presents its redemptive message of hope to you and me.

David Sanford
Book Publishing Consultant
Author of Loving *Your Neighbor: Surprise!*
It's Not What You Think

Lynn Hare embraces her humanity while experiencing the power and mystery of a transformation possible through self-forgiveness. She appropriates truth for herself but does not come away with pat answers. *The Quest for Self-Forgiveness* is a useful resource for all who want release from the bondage accompanying the lack of forgiveness. Lynn's journey towards self-forgiveness is open, humble, and authentic as she explores what it means to have a vibrant relationship with Christ.

Dr. Thomas and Bonnie Kopp
Paraclete Mission Group
www.paraclete.net/kopp

It is far too easy to look back on the failures of our past and relive the pain and consequences of our poor choices. Self-condemnation can haunt even the best of us. Lynn Hare's honesty, humility, and humor in her book *Quest for Self-Forgiveness* is Holy Spirit-inspired.

Each reader gets drawn in as Lynn shares her personal journey: "I was convinced I would someday open the 'closet' of my failures and the entire wardrobe would come crashing onto my head. Hats. Belts. Umbrellas. Thunk! Thunk! Thunk!" Lynn invites us to join her in an adventure to freedom from our self-condemning thought lives. Forgiveness is truly the key we've all been looking for.

Chad McComas
Editor of *The Christian Journal* newspaper
thechristianjournal.org

There are not many people that cross our lives that stop you in your tracks. Lynn Hare is that kind of person. The depth of her soul, the love in her heart, and the wisdom of her mind point to Jesus over and over again.

With biblical truths, the Holy Spirit flows from her heart, and through her own walk-through of tough issues, Lynn brings a spring of fresh water to refresh and enlighten any person with a challenge in front of them.

God has gifted Lynn with a life of extraordinary wisdom. Her words are based on the foundational truths of the word of God, and those words are translated into tangible love.

I am blessed to say I have been challenged and changed by this extraordinary woman.

I highly recommend her book *The Quest for Self-Forgiveness.* The grace of Jesus flows through Lynn Hare, and you will be moved and changed by her examples brought to light in this book.

Bonnie Knopf
Contemporary Christian Songwriter and Artist
www.bonnieknopf.com

Lynn writes from the heart. I enjoyed walking through her story. As a counselor, I have found no other book on self-forgiveness that encourages people to interact with the material. I value the Scripture references to guide the experience.

Self-forgiveness is one of the hardest tasks we face as humans and I have sat with many people over the years that are unable to think through this concept. I now have a tool to use with my clients. Lynn, thank you for your courage to write this book. I know that people will be blessed and lives will be changed.

Nadine Dody
Licensed Professional Counselor
www.nadinedodylpc.com

I thank Lynn for writing this much-needed, important book! Lynn's beautiful transparency and vulnerability in her book opens up a new world for us so that as we partake in her journey, we learn important truths from her life that will change us forever. Lynn inspires her readers to rise up in boldness and courage to face their past and outlines simple principles so they can experience the hope, healing, and freedom that results from self-forgiveness. I highly recommend this book to everyone. You will not be the same. As you read this book, receive the hope, healing, and freedom that you have longed for!

Ruth Lum
Executive Assistant to the President & Chairman/CEO
Secretary to the Board of Directors
Kingdom Congressional International Alliance (KCIA)
www.kcialliance.org

In *The Quest for Self-Forgiveness*, I experienced the mind of Christ—the truth of God inscribed in Lynn's heart. She explains her struggles and how God healed the broken places, restored her with His lovingkindness, and healed the pain, guilt, and shame.

With laughter, humorous stories, and a light-hearted voice, Lynn shares how God worked in her to change the landscape of her soul as He miraculously worked within her heart. Lynn sets you up to rest in the peace of God's restorative power. I recommend this book to anyone suffering from the pain of hope deferred. It will open up your heart to the realization of the power of God to heal.

Alexis Alexander
In His Image Ministries Transformation

Lynn Hare's *Quest for Self-Forgiveness* is a fresh and God-breathed approach to walking through self-forgiveness. I admire her transparency, strength, and humility. Her step-by-step discovery into self-forgiveness models how you can walk through trauma in your life, encounter the presence of God and His amazing, radical love, and come out an overcomer.

Lynn makes it easy to understand how to forgive yourself and that through this process, you learn to love yourself. Experience your own freedom as you are released to walk in your true identity—the way God sees you.

Anna Chacon Funke
Inner Healing and Deliverance Ministry

This book assures us there's no reason to let guilt continue to rule our lives. By being real, Lynn Hare tells of her struggles and how the lies that held her hostage were quieted. From a woman who knows first-hand what it means to discover self-forgiveness, we find hope to release our own self-condemning thoughts, past wrongs, poor choices, lies of the enemy, and embrace our true worth.

We, too, can step into the relaxed, freed-up life we long to experience. This book is a gem that takes readers, one exercise at a time, into the amazing benefits of self-forgiveness.

The Quest for Self-Forgiveness

Maxine Marsolini
Former President, Oregon Christian Writers
Co-host of *The River* blog talk radio
Author of *Mother's Fury, Rebuilding Families One Dollar at a Time*, and *Raising Children in Blended Families*
Founder of Rebuilding Families
www.rebuildingfamilies.net

If you've got the notion that mistakes you've made define who you are now, think again, says Lynn Hare, in her powerful and personal book, *The Quest for Self-Forgiveness*. Filled with understanding of the human struggle to forgive yourself, she reveals how you can move from guilt and shame to a fresh awareness of who you are *now*. If you're living with painful self-accusation, *The Quest for Self-Forgiveness* will bring healing and hope to your heart. Don't wait to begin this essential and life-empowering journey with Lynn and the Holy Spirit.

Poppy Smith
Inspirational Speaker
Award-winning Author
Christian Life Coach
www.poppysmith.com

Table of Contents

Section Four
Healing: Find Your Safe Place

Section Five
Godly Perspective: Take Back the Past

Section Six
Overcoming: Taste Victory

Section Seven
Community: Foster Forgiveness

Appendixes

Foreword

On a flight from Sacramento, a woman talked excitedly about her trip to see grandkids in Alaska. Seated to my right, she kept trying to turn to face me as we talked—but every few seconds had to turn away and rotate her neck or shoulders. The pain and restriction were obvious, but she soldiered on.

"Are you in pain?" I asked. She nodded and told me her story. "Last winter, most workers at our dairy farm and my husband were down with the flu. The cows must be milked, and I was the only one healthy enough to try. By the end of the day, they were all milked, but I was hurt in ways that my doctor, my chiropractor, and my massage therapist cannot seem to resolve."

I felt her pain, and heard a whisper, "She needs to forgive herself." I offered to fix her pain, and when she asked how I planned to do that, I said "magic."

Keep in mind, dear reader, that I am a believer in Jesus—not in magic. But some people grow up believing in those three "magic words" that open doors of opportunity: "Please! Thank you! You are welcome!" The beautiful thing about this kind of magic is that it always works, regardless of your age, race, education, gender, or social status.

So it is with self-forgiveness.

I asked her to repeat four magic words aloud: "I now forgive myself." As she did, her joints and muscles snapped, crackled and popped like the famous bowl of Rice Krispies encountering cold milk. In less than a minute, she tested each of the areas where she had had restricted movement and

i

pain—neck, shoulders, back and arms—and found them to be unrestricted and pain-free! During the remainder of our flight, we discussed the same principles found in this new book by Lynn Hare.

In the years that followed, hundreds of people of great faith and of no faith have found new freedom from distress of all kinds through self-forgiveness.

Lynn's 20-year journey to forgive herself for the distracted driving that caused severe injury to her baby boy Ben is real. You can trust Lynn—she has proven these principles in daily living for herself, and has brought others into marvelous freedom along the way.

Of course, there are more people to forgive and often we need to seek forgiveness from God and from other people, but it all begins with self-forgiveness.

I hope that you'll take time now, and each day, to utter a sincere declaration: "I now forgive myself."

Journey together with Lynn, and see for yourself how exciting and liberating it can be.

John Anderson
President
Global Development Partners Group Ltd.
www.gdpgrp.com

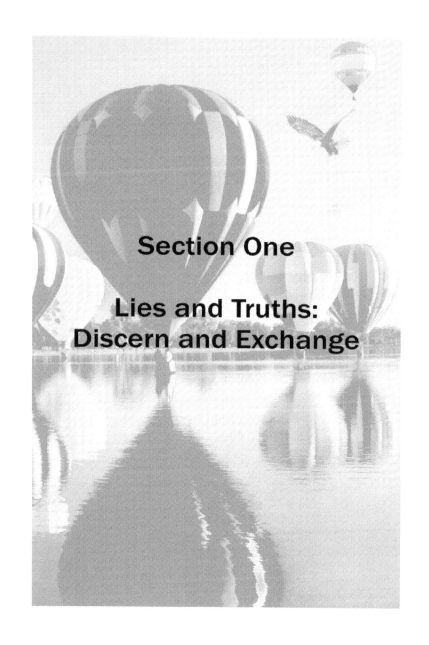

Section One

Lies and Truths:
Discern and Exchange

Introduction

Milpitas, California, July 1988

"Let's go, Baby Ben. Time to hang out with our friends. We've dropped your dad off at work. Sky's clear. Traffic on the freeway up ahead looks pretty light. What's that noise? Oh, you've fallen asleep holding your rattle.

"If I leave that rattle in your hand, the noise will wake you up."

I took my eyes off the road and reached across the infant car seat to pull the orange and yellow rattle from my son's fist.

Whomp! My subcompact car jumped the curb and crunched into a light pole, leveling it. My face bounced off the steering wheel. Searing pain shot up my right leg.

Four-month-old Ben's explosive cry pierced the morning air, but I couldn't move to help him. My right foot was trapped, crushed in the floorboards of the car.

A man pulled to the side of the road and punched 911 into his cell phone.

A middle-aged woman stopped and leapt from her car. Leaning through the open window, she asked, "How can I help you?"

"Pray with me!" I cried as I clenched her hand. I stuttered, "G-God, help! Please don't let B-Ben have b-brain damage!"

She shot an alarmed glance at him and gasped, "Look at your baby!"

What had first appeared to be a slight bruise on the side of his head now bulged like a watermelon.

Paramedics arrived and extracted us from the wreckage. With the Jaws of Life, they pried the floorboards apart and released my foot from the accelerator pedal.

Once inside the ambulance, my back pressed against the coarse canvas of a stretcher beside Ben, I clutched his tiny hand. His wail almost drowned out the ambulance's siren as we raced to San Jose Medical Center. At the hospital, orderlies swept us into the ER. Questions and commands flurried across us. I lost sight of Ben as they rushed me into surgery to repair my fractured, dislocated foot that had bones at strange rakish angles like step stairs.

The next day, I lay recovering in a hospital room, exhausted. My husband, Tim, came in and sat down beside the bed. We discussed the accident, and I described the intense pain in my foot, chest, and back. My stomach twisting, I asked, "How's Ben?"

"He's in the ICU, two floors above us, fighting bad fevers. They put him in an induced coma."

"What does the doctor say?"

"He's on his way."

The staccato of heels on hard tiles telegraphed his arrival.

"Mr. and Mrs. Hare," the surgeon said. He paused. "I'm

afraid I have some bad news. The CT scans show your son has a fractured skull and brain damage."

I squeezed Tim's hand. "How bad is it?" I asked.

Frowning, he glanced at his clipboard. "Damage to 25, maybe 33 percent of the right brain."

I drew in a sharp breath. "Is he going to be okay?"

"His left eye, arm, and leg aren't functioning. We'll do more tests to determine the next step."

The color drained from Tim's face. After the doctor left, we prayed a short, faltering prayer. Tim went upstairs to visit our son.

Two weeks later, sweet Baby Ben still lay in the ICU in a medically-induced coma, in a tangle of tubes, breathing machines, and IVs. I left the hospital in a wheelchair, longing for Ben to join me.

Once home, I camped out on a small bed in the middle of the living room. I shifted my cast-bound foot and gazed across the room at a photo of my dimpled, beaming boy.

"I love that picture of Baby Ben." I winced. "But today, he's not smiling. He isn't even conscious."

We prayed that a bed would open for Ben at Stanford University Hospital. But nearby San Francisco hospital staffs were on strike, so Stanford beds were at a premium. Ben's raging fevers and the hematoma on the right side of his head grew. Finally, we got the long-awaited call: a room had opened up at Stanford. He was immediately scheduled for surgery.

A neurosurgeon performed a four-hour operation to repair the lining of Ben's brain. A couple of days later, the doctors allowed Ben to wake up.

With his surgery incision held in place by 32 staples

covered with a huge gauze turban, Ben drew smiles as nurses took him along on their rounds, pulling him in a little red wagon. Soon he ate his first baby food from a jar.

Requests for healing went out on prayer chains to thousands. We contended for Ben's life.

> **Pain insists upon being attended to. God whispers to us in our pleasures, speaks in our conscience, but shouts in our pain: it is His megaphone to rouse a deaf world.**[1]
> ~ **C.S. Lewis**

His seizures slowed and then stopped. He was released to come home. We cheered when he arrived. Once I regained my strength, my stamina to walk, drive, and take care of the household returned. But every phone call made my stomach lurch, and a mallet pounded a bass drum inside my chest. Guilt leaned in, hissing, "See what you've done? Irreversible. Unforgivable."

I quickly shoved it into a suitcase in my mind and slammed the lid shut. But a bit hung out through the cracks, like the edges of a sleeve.

I desperately needed to forgive myself. Could I that week? No. That month? No. Not that year, or the year after, or even the year after that. It took more than *20 years* to release myself from the guilt of the car accident that had hurt my son.

For 28 years, I've prayed one-on-one with thousands of people. I've found that, in the middle of heartbreak, anger, and fear, one thing held most of them back from breakthrough: they couldn't appropriate God's grace for

themselves.

You will find within these pages truths I discovered about self-forgiveness as I struggled to find God in the middle of self-made chaos. My prayer is that you'll encounter a forgiving God who loves you deeply, no matter what differences you might be reconciling with Him.

I extend to you an invitation to accept yourself with renewed grace. I wish I'd had a book like this in my hands to help me navigate the painful process of coming to peace with myself. I'm eager for you to know the profound love of our Heavenly Father, who believes in you and wants you to believe in yourself, too.

How to Use This Book

Each chapter includes insights about self-forgiveness, a bit of my personal journey, a core truth, and a prayer. After reading each chapter, I suggest that you pray the prayer aloud. You'll get the most out of this book by completing the practical activities called "Take the Next Step" to advance you on your path of self-forgiveness. Go on an explore and check out the appendixes at the back of the book. There you'll find a prayer to Make Jesus Your Best Friend, my Daily Prayer, Scripture Verses about Our Identity in Christ, Recommended Reading, and a recap of the Core Truths.

As you read this book, expect God to reach into the deep, dark mines of your soul that no one else has been able to touch. He will bring a lantern there and lead you up and out to sunlight-bathed clearings of freedom and grace.

Let the Holy Spirit be your guide on this journey of freedom without following a formula in the process. The

5

ideas within these pages are meant as springboards for a unique trajectory with Him. Allow the arc of that path to take its natural course—one word, one thought, one experience at a time. Frame that with your own perspective.

Celebrate your relationship with the Holy Spirit and expect to know Him in a deeper, richer, and fuller way. Each day is a new beginning in Him for you. As you reach out to God, expect supernatural shifts in your heart and mind. He'll honor that. Say, "God, I give you my heart. How will You work all of this out?"

Expect outrageous encounters with the brilliant Redeemer. He has seen everything you've been through. *Everything.* And He never wastes pain. *Never.* He can take anything and everything you've been through and make it into raw beauty. He has this funny way of using even the most peculiar things for His glory.

Get ready to be uplifted in His time. Remember that God sees your heart. God sees *you.*

I have prayed for you, dear reader, for many years. I expect that every step of the way, you will find fresh God-truths that resonate in your soul. Together let's celebrate the brilliant Redeemer!

Friend, whatever weighs on your heart and mind, our Heavenly Father has already forgiven you. I invite you to forgive yourself—body, soul, and spirit. Give it a go. Give it to Him. He can and will redeem it all.

I dare you to go on a quest for self-forgiveness.

---

[1]C.S. Lewis. *The Problem of Pain.* HarperCollins. 1996. p. 91.

Where You've Been
Is Not Who You Are

*Forget the former things; do not dwell on
the past. See, I am doing a new thing! Now it
springs up; do you not perceive it?*

Isaiah 43:18–19

If nothing goes wrong, it's not an adventure. I'm a big fan
of adventure!

The Bible is full of daring exploits. In Damascus, Paul
was lowered in a basket through the opening in a wall. He
lived through prison terms, a shipwreck, and snake bites.
Joseph spent years behind bars for a crime he didn't commit.
Noah's floating zoo surged over the seas for more than a
year. Daniel faced death in a lion's pit because of loyalty to
his Deliverer.

It seems like every day is wild for me, too. But my
adventures happen not so much because of my faithfulness,
but rather are results of mistakes I've made. Not a day goes
by without one. Quest for adventure: game on!

God knows that sometimes we can't predict the results

of our own foolishness. The journey of forgiving our own missteps can get perilous. Where does the danger lie? In trying to reconcile our past with who we are.

Bound for . . . Where?

Imagine buying a magic ticket for a cruise. The moment the ticket was placed in your hand, you could immediately sense the sights, sounds, and smells of your destination.

Suppose you boarded an ocean liner in New York City bound for London. As you climb the ramp and step onto the deck of the ship in New York, you sense a mist of light showers; a cart clattering over London cobblestones; smoke wafting to you from the entrance to the subway; and the aroma of onion, garlic, dried fish, and pepper rising to you from the shops that flank the roadway where pedestrians dart into the path of impatient cabbies.

God sees like that. God sees forward.

Our past tells us where we *were*. But where we've been doesn't define us any more than a baseball bat in a rowboat makes it an oar or a fly swatter in a kitchen makes it a spatula.

All of heaven pours out its Spirit on who we're becoming. The Lord wants us to reframe our past. In the reframe, He says, "It's time to forgive yourself."

Sometimes, we look back on an event and think, "I should have known better. Jumped higher. Thought things through a little more." Yeah, maybe.

But I have a feeling that God understood our overwhelm at the time, and He has a deeper compassion for us than we have for ourselves. He gets it. He knows everything about us. And when *He* looks at what happened, He wants us to quit beating ourselves up. As He reviews our lives, you can bet He's saying, "It's time to forgive yourself."

Sleepless Nights

For most of my life, as I turned in for the night, my thoughts churned like the outboard motor of a speedboat. I tossed and turned, reviewing mental DVDs of my mistakes from that day. Sometimes I'd yelled at my kids. I'd yelled at Tim. I'd yelled at myself.

For years, whenever the memory of the car accident with Ben flashed across the screen of my mind, I cringed. I saw myself leaning across the car seat to pull the rattle out of his hand. In horror, I looked up just in time to see a light pole coming at us. I felt the impact of the car wrapping around the light pole and striking it to the ground. That mistake cost Ben a fractured skull and brain damage. The memory of his shrill howl kept me awake for hours.

I was furious with myself. Flashbacks formed a clover leaf of repeating, dizzying curves. The years that followed the accident tested my faith, my parenthood, and my commitment to a Savior who seemed nowhere in sight.

I knew I needed to move forward, but I was bewildered as to how to do that. I knew better than to talk to myself with contempt, but I couldn't figure out how to get that to register in the little gray cells in my head.

A Common Experience

Then something curious happened. When I shared my story, people told me they beat themselves up, too. I spoke to ministers of the gospel, authors, homemakers, prison inmates, teachers, students, personal coaches—people from every walk of life.

When they brought up mistakes from their past, they all had something in common: they were convinced that the errors from their past defined them. They called themselves "stupid," "slow," "lazy," and "crazy." When I prayed, I told them that God doesn't call them those names. His power shows up in His lovingkindness. He focuses on who we are and where we're going.

If you've got the notion that some mistake you've made defines who you are, think again. Reach forward.

> *A mistake is a teacher, not a disciplinarian. A protagonist, not an antagonist. An opportunist, not a defeatist. A detour, not a brick wall. An equal opportunity employer.*

Agree with the God Who Sees All about what lies ahead. Because you can pull *that* reality into *today*.

Yes, you'll still make mistakes. If there were no risk, there'd be no adventure! But you and I can celebrate our zealous quest with the ultimate Adventurer Himself.

Failure doesn't mean you have accomplished nothing.
It does mean you have learned something.
Failure doesn't mean you have been a fool.
It does mean you had a lot of faith.
Failure doesn't mean you've been disgraced.
It does mean you were willing to try.

Failure doesn't mean you don't have it.
It does mean you have to do something
in a different way.
Failure doesn't mean you are inferior.
It does mean you are not perfect.
Failure doesn't mean you've wasted your life.
It does mean you have a reason to start afresh.
Failure doesn't mean you'll never make it.
It does mean it will take a little longer.
Failure doesn't mean God has abandoned you.
It does mean God has a better idea!
~ *Robert Schuller*[1]

Core Truth: Our past does not define us.

Let's Pray

Holy Spirit, as I reach ahead with supernatural forward-thinking, turn the pages for me, especially on days when I have no idea what comes next. Show me how to frame this chapter in my book of life in terms of what lies ahead: wins of godly success. You dream forward. And with You, so do I.

Take my faults, failures, and frustrations and turn them into strengths, successes, and certainties. With a fresh understanding of who You are, I choose to forgive myself. As You reveal Yourself to me in my pain, show me how to draw on Your love and mercy. Who am I becoming in You?

Take the Next Step

Sketch an adventure you've had and another that illustrates one you'd like to have in the future.

Beneath each picture, write one word or phrase that describes who you are in the adventure, such as "wilderness camper" or "world traveler" or "inner-city pioneer." Place the sketches where you can see them often. How can the adventurer in the first sketch move you toward the adventure in the second?

---

[1]Robert Schuller, *You Can Become the Person You Want to Be.* New York: Hawthorn Books, Inc. 1973. p. 73.

Relax into Mistakes,
No Matter the Size

Above all, keep loving one another earnestly,
since love covers a multitude of sins.

1 Peter 4:8 (ESV)

It's time to be brutally frank. I've got mistakes down to an art.

On our first date, Tim and I sat a dozen rows apart at a movie. I'd spent so much time in the restroom that by the time I arrived in the dark theater, the movie had already begun. I dropped into a seat in the back row and watched the film from there.

A couple of weeks later, at my apartment, I heated up a pot of water on the stove, planning to make hard-boiled eggs. Tim and I sat down to watch a movie, and I forgot about the water. A while later, I smelled smoke and raced to an empty pot belching black clouds into the kitchen.

I've shrunk half a dozen sweaters by throwing them in the dryer on the high setting. They became so small, they would have fit a Yorkshire terrier.

I once backed my SUV out of the garage and smashed

the side-view mirror on the wall. I dented the fender and picked up streaks of paint by scraping the side of the car against our house's cedar siding. *Gulp.*

I turned on a stove burner beneath an empty glass lasagna pan and stepped into the living room to text a friend. The pan exploded, showering the kitchen with hundreds of projectiles that seared the floor and left it with permanent red scars.

Oops.

Not all my mistakes have been harmless mishaps. Tim and I have three bright, fun-loving kids—Ben, Andy, and Emily. For the longest time, I thought I'd left scars on their hearts, too, with my harsh words and condescending messages.

Family Reunion

I used to try to hide my gaffes, but now I make a conscious effort to admit them. At a family reunion to celebrate my parents' 55th anniversary, a few of us shared DVDs we'd made to honor them. Mine featured photos, clips of songs and movies, and nostalgic stories. Although the family politely watched the main footage, their attention snapped to the screen as the outtakes kicked into action. I called Superman "Kent Clark." The ice cubes in a glass of tea wouldn't budge when I tried to stir them. I sang *Everyone Knows It's Wendy* with a mosquito dancing across my forehead. The family laughed and applauded as they watched one gaffe after another.

As a recovering perfectionist, I enjoyed the moment as much as they did. Sharing the goof-ups was my way of saying, "Let's laugh together at our shortcomings." We can celebrate our mistakes because our Redeemer is in those moments. When we release acceptance of ourselves and our families by openly sharing our faults, grace is released in our homes. And when that happens, we make our families a safe place to grow.

A Stadium Full of Mistakes

Honestly, if the mistakes I've made were hot dogs, you could wolf down a Wrigley Field full on a Saturday night and still have plenty left over for breakfast. And as hard as I try, I'm not always able to hit a home run when I try to forgive myself for those blunders.

I like to think about grace as a baseball game. I mentally challenge myself to get out of the batting cage and pick up the worn, wooden bat and release my self-blame. But some days, I can hardly imagine making it to first base. I'm not even sure if my cleats are on the right feet!

I used to think, "Sure, it's easy to forgive the small stuff, but what about huge offenses?" As I got to know the Savior, I was relieved to find that He had this thing figured out. To Him, offenses don't carry different weights. They're all the same. Each and every one is forgiven.

Envision Jesus as your divine Pitcher. He sends a ball across the plate. Do you see times when you failed to connect with the ball, and your Pitcher always had another opportunity waiting? Christ never despairs over your misses but immediately forgives you and keeps trying to help you get a hit. You always have another chance to hit one out of the park. What can you do to help yourself see your hits and

> **For Jesus, when it comes to grace, a grand slam is just as easy as a single.**

misses the way He sees them?

You know, love covers a multitude of sins, including love we extend to ourselves. If we welcome imperfection each time we blow it, we have the chance to experience acceptance for ourselves and others. That makes it easier to have kinder self-talk and to chuckle with Jesus-joy at dented fenders and Chihuahua sweaters. When that happens and laughter rises up and out of us, we become more like Him.

Go ahead. Step up to the plate. And swing!

Core Truth: Mistakes are opportunities to grow in self-acceptance.

Let's Pray

Jesus, take my failures and release them from me. Restore my emotions to the way You created them. Take away my self-directed offenses—big, medium, and small—and replace them with Your deep love. I purpose right now to extend acceptance to myself. Holy Spirit, thank You for filling me with joy, forgiveness, and a sense of humor to see me through. I forgive myself. Game on!

Take the Next Step

Draw a picture of yourself batting in the Major League playoffs. Label a ball coming across the plate with a goal you had in the past. Swing! You miss. Label a second ball flying across the plate with another past goal. Swing! You miss again.

Take a minute to ask Jesus how He defines success and give the third ball that label. Swing! Draw yourself knocking the ball out of the park. What does gaining Christ's perspective release in the process of forgiving yourself?

Journal Your
Forgiveness Journey

I will remember the deeds of the Lord.
Psalm 77:11 (ESV)

The more time we spend with the Lord in intimacy, the more we begin to think like He thinks and love like He loves. But sometimes, loving ourselves doesn't come easily. That happens when we spend time in the transforming presence of the Lord. He desires mature love in us.

God doesn't just love. God *is* love. And if He is love, everything He does displays His affection. He creates in love. He speaks with love. He protects in love.

The beauty of the relationship is that Christ lives in us. Even though our bodies are subject to death because of sin, the Spirit gives life because of righteousness (Romans 8:10). We need to interact with God-truths and to document the rich experiences that bring them home.

A critical part of forgiving yourself is taking inventory of your growth over time. One of the best ways is to journal your journey. Here are some tips to track your progress.

1. **Date each entry.** Later, you'll be able to trace your growth to chronological markers connected with milestones that show when shifts took place.

2. **Write out three things you're grateful for.** The Holy One inhabits the praise of His people (see Psalm 22:3). This means that He lives in our words that express gratitude. Look for Him in the simplest things: an encouraging email, a friend's phone call, or a child's dandelion. Be creative! How is He blessing you? Write it down.

3. **Ask the Holy Spirit for a passage to make your own.** Copy down one key thought or Scripture that captures your attention or resonates in your heart. What do you identify with? When He speaks to us, the Holy Spirit will give us personal prophecy for the purpose of edifying, exhorting, and comforting (see 1 Corinthians 14:3). When we journal about what He's revealing in these three areas, it builds our faith in the power of His love.

4. **Ask a question and write down the Holy Spirit's response in the moment of spontaneous flow.** *"Do not conform to the pattern of this world, but be transformed by the renewing of your mind. Then you will be able to test and approve what God's will is—his good, pleasing and perfect will"* (Romans 12:2). When your thoughts are transformed, you'll *"think of yourself with sober judgment, in accordance with the faith God has distributed to . . . you"* (Romans 12:3). Your Renewer loves *your* growth. Your Renewer loves *you*.

    So what if your journal pages are messy or filled with incomplete thoughts? Writing—even when you ramble—

gives a voice to your emotions and spirit. I recommend an outstanding book on two-way journaling called *4 Keys to Hearing God's Voice* by Mark and Patti Virkler. They provide detailed steps on how to listen for His voice and journal what you hear.[1]

Over and over, I've asked questions. I lost a daughter to stillbirth. I had nasty conflicts with Tim. I lost sleep praying for a friend with cancer. I poured out my personal grief onto journal pages and recorded dialogues with the Trinity in the throne room. God is always there. The deepest wound. The longest scar. The tear-streaked pages. That's where the Lord is doing some of His best work.

5. **As you pray, envision Jesus, not the problem. Ask Him, "What are You up to in this?"** Clear your mind and look for Jesus in your situation.

6. **Take time to reflect.** Refine your questions. As you grow to know the Holy Spirit better, upgrade the nature of your reflections. Get excited when you pose questions that reflect a broader sense of what the Holy Spirit is doing in your life.

7. **Expect *"Aha!"* moments**. In His sovereignty, the Lord loves to surprise us with personal revelations that quicken our hearts. Look for them. Expect them. *"Aha!"* moments are sheer platinum. When the home team lost, how did they demonstrate victory? How did a death bring home a broader sense of Christ's life? When you experienced deep disappointment, where was His glory displayed? Give incongruities a chance to become the meshing gears of personal progress.

8. Pay attention to repeated impressions or key phrases.
"Once God has spoken; twice have I heard this: that power belongs to God" (Psalm 62:11 ESV). When He repeats an idea, phrase, name, Scripture, or precept, He's often calling our attention to His will and giving us confirmation. What themes recur on our journal pages? What shifts do they indicate?

> God is faithful to His promises. So as you take the steps to forgive yourself, you can be strong and courageous.[2]

9. Write down prayers, promises, and Scriptures others have prayed or spoken into you. Include nicknames and identities God has given. Was there a key name, phrase, or idea? *"There is a God in heaven who reveals secrets"* (Daniel 2:28 NKJV). What is the Holy Spirit revealing?

10. Revisit the pages of your journal. Sometimes an answer to prayer isn't found in today's devotional time. It might be in a promise you heard last month or last year. Look back over the pages and track promises and answers to prayer. Reread your journal pages monthly.

11. Share truths you discover with a mentor or other trusted friend. What resonates? Together, what are you discovering about the nature of Him who is called Faithful and True?

12. Look for the Savior's goodness woven through the pages. *"'For I know the plans I have for you,' declares the LORD, 'plans to prosper you and not to harm you, plans to give you hope and a future'"* (Jeremiah 29:11).

Exploring Word Play

I invite you to take a peek inside the pages of my journals. Here are a few features you'll see.

A-Z gratitude lists: I write the alphabet vertically on the left side of the page—"A" at the top to "Z" at the bottom. I list things I'm grateful for that begin with each letter.

Acronyms: I like to play with words. I write out the letters of an emotionally-charged word and spell out a fresh meaning using each letter. For example, when I felt like I was trying to do things on my own (and failing miserably), I winced whenever I heard the word "control." So I wrote down the left side of my journal page: C.O.N.T.R.O.L. I assigned a word to each letter: "Christ Overcomes Now, Triumphant Roar Of Lion!" Then, whenever I encountered that word, I had a new mental "hook" to connect it to.

Coined words: If I can't find words that express how I feel, I make them up. I "blankify" calendar pages to spend time with Jesus. When I'm "willie-niverred," I ask God to help me move forward out of feeling emotionally stuck. And when I've got plenty of energy to bounce through the day, I ask God how best to use my "energistic" zeal.

Personalized pages: I write my name in Scriptures. I listen for God to speak and add my name to the strength and power He breathes through the passages. *"Fear not, for I have redeemed Lynn; I have called Lynn by name, she is mine"* (Isaiah 43:1 ESV). Writing it out makes it personal. That's what intimacy is all about—deep, private moments with our First Love.

Humor breaks: I wrote out the story in Luke 7 of Jesus healing a man in a town called Nain. His mother grieved her loss. Jesus drew alongside the dead man being carried in a coffin and prayed for him. The man came to life. I wondered what the young man might have said as he sat up and looked around.

"Okay, whose idea was the coffin? We were praying for a miracle, right?"

"Jesus, thanks! Hug?"

"Who would like prayer right now? I've got faith for healing."

"Anyone capture this on your smartphone? This *so* needs to go out on Facebook."

"Okay, who walked off with my shoes?"

Speech bubbles: I write out dialogues with Father God, Jesus, or the Holy Spirit. I use their names as I write. The words appear in speech bubbles that alternate from one side of the page to the other—mine, then theirs.

Poetry: Some poems rhyme. Most don't. Some are gentle, flowing words that cascade across the pages. Others are raw, exposed pain that zigzag without much logic or even cadence. Sometimes I write poems meant for Jesus alone.

Jagged page edges where entries used to be: I like to revisit journal pages, but sometimes the words and images I've recorded stir up resentment for myself or other people. While some journal passages justify another look, others simply need to go. So I tear out the pages and let go of the memories, trusting that if I need to recall anything later, the

Redeemer will bring it back to mind in His time.

Small boxes that say "next." I sometimes miss a day or two of journaling; later, when I resume, I need a reminder of where I left off. At the end of my quiet time, I make a small box on the side of the page, reminding myself of what I want to accomplish in the next session, such as the next verse in a passage I'm studying, a key word or phrase, or a thought I want to finish.

Even on your most discouraging days, your heavenly Father wraps His love around you. He's got a master plan, and you can do nothing to destroy it. As you reflect on your journal entries, you're likely to find assurance that His goodness waits for you ahead.

Core Truth: Tracking our growth by journaling can help us mark the upward path on our journeys of self-forgiveness.

Let's Pray

Holy Spirit, I remove distractions and quiet my soul before You. What are You thinking? What are You feeling? Here is a blank journal page. Possibilities are exploding wide open! Father, I'm listening for Your voice. Jesus, I'm seeking Your face. Holy Spirit, I'm sensing Your presence.

With my Bible in hand, I enter into Your presence, trusting You implicitly. Release God-truths, and I'll write them down. Thank You for the process of maturity that grows me to become more like You!

Take the Next Step

Begin a journal. Write a Bible verse that resonates in your heart and personalize it with your name. Use at least one idea from this chapter in your journal. What shift is taking place in your self-acceptance as you focus on God's Word?

Ask the Holy Spirit, "How can I journal creatively?" Listen for the response while you write and later, as you reread and ponder what you have written.

---

[1]Mark and Patti Virkler. *4 Keys to Hearing God's Voice*. Destiny Image. 2010. pp. 213-251.

[2]Dr. Bruce Wilkinson and Mark E. Strong. *The Freedom Factor: Finding Peace by Forgiving Others . . . and Yourself*. Zeal Books. 2016. p. 128.

Chronicle Growth with
Creative Illustrations

I will ponder all your work,
and meditate on your mighty deeds.

Psalm 77:12 (ESV)

When our three kids, Ben, Andy and Emily, were preschoolers, we often pored over the pages of picture Bibles. The illustrations leapt from the page with vivid color. Jonah prayed inside the belly of a bouncing whale on churning sea swells. Daniel bowed his head in the lions' den where an angel came and shut the ravenous beasts' mouths. Jesus rode through town on the back of a donkey, and palm branches swept him through the streets of Jerusalem.

The kids sometimes laughed and pointed to the illustrations. They said, "I want to be in that picture!" They recognized that inside the joy of each story was the miracle of God's presence.

When reading a Bible passage, picture yourself in the story. Join the apostles in the upper room. Is your soul stirred by the flames of fire over the disciples' heads? Drink in

Jesus' Spirit. What are you feeling? Are you weeping? Are you joyful? Both? What does Christ convey to you with His voice? His hands? His eyes?

> *Jesus' creativity bursts through shafts of a foothill's first dawnlight. One stroke of His paintbrush on a canvas stirs 1,000 angels to flight.*

As you chronicle your growth, include images the Holy Spirit provides. When we find and record images that reflect the Kingdom, we move in His power. Jesus told 46 parables that depicted His Kingdom in living color. We can creatively design pictures that bring His truths to life, too.

- **Draw an image on the page without analyzing it.** The Holy Spirit sometimes gives an image without explaining it. Go with it and record the picture as it comes to you. Do you see a waterfall? A double-arched bridge? A city on a hill? A cornfield? An apple orchard? Draw the impression that comes to mind.

- **Make a quick sketch**. Don't sweat your art skills. Draw stick figures if you need to. Illustrate Scripture with online images, such as clipart. A recent entry in my journal was about releasing regret and pressing toward the prize. I wrote, *"Run in such a way as to get the prize"* (1 Corinthians 9:24). I googled "clipart runner," and copied by hand the image of a runner with upraised arms at the finish line. There are lots of resources with free domain images to print. Focus on capturing Christ's heart. What's He feeling? What's He conveying to you in the process? What are you feeling?

- **Get creative!** Bring images to life with a variety of media. Explore colored pencils, paint, chalk, silkscreen, clay, or tapestry. You can illustrate Holy Spirit encounters in a thousand ways. Consider sharing your artwork on social media with a line or two of what He revealed.

- **Snap a picture or take a video.** What pictures or videos have you taken recently? A double rainbow? A sandpiper on the beach? The glassy reflection of a mountain on a lake? Use smartphone apps to record images and a word or two that come to mind.

Splash Color onto the Pages

Here are snapshots of a few illustrations in my journals:
- **Pie charts:** Eight-slice pie charts serve as handy graphic organizers for key precepts.

- **Fun animals, bridges, and adventures:** I sketch with bright pencils to illustrate metaphors—the more colorful, the better. Pictures with bright hues are likely to enter our minds with emotions attached, which makes them easier to remember later.

- **Bodies of water:** Water in the Bible usually represents the presence of the Holy Spirit. I've filled page after page with rivers, streams, seas, ponds, and fountains.

- **Silly illustrations:** At a school where I taught, staff members I lunched with wouldn't warm up to discussions about God. When I talked about my faith, a spirit of ridicule mocked me. When I asked Jesus what He saw, He reminded me, *"Do not throw your pearls before swine"* (Matthew 7:6 NASB). In my journal, I drew a big pearl with an itty-bitty pig sprawled across the top.

- **Pictures of Jesus:** Christ walking the dusty roads of Jerusalem; deep conversation with the Samaritan woman at the well; on the cross; resurrected; crunching gravel beneath his sandaled feet; smiling at a child on His shoulders; peering through binoculars.

Look for Patterns

- **Join pictures together as they come to you.** Stages of spiritual and emotional growth don't always happen in sequential order. In fact, a lot times, they zigzag or maybe spiral upward like an ascending staircase. One image might lead to the next without a logical progression. That's fine. Stay in the flow of the imagery. The Holy Spirit is creative and loves to explore!

- **Maintain journal pages on apps and access them on multiple devices.** As you collect images, add, change, and rearrange as you go along.

- **Note similar themes that recur.** They'll likely show areas of supernatural growth that the Holy Spirit is targeting. What is He saying to your heart?

- **Revisit your journal pages regularly.** What past promises are being fulfilled in the natural right now? Soak in the Holy Spirit's presence. Relax and review pictures you've co-created with Him in the past and see how they connect to today's and tomorrow's plans.

Core Truth: Our self-forgiveness journeys have more impact with creative illustrations.

Let's Pray

Jesus, show me creative ways to capture Your truth with pictures, photos, illustrations, and other forms of art. What do You see? I see it, too. Open the eyes of my heart for future possibilities. I will revisit these pages as You direct me back to the beauty we've co-created within.

Take the Next Step

On your next journal page, use one idea from this chapter and illustrate what the Holy Spirit reveals. What emotions come up as the picture comes to life? What is He releasing in the process? Ask Him, "How can I creatively depict my transitions and growth?"

Exchange Each Lie for Its Truth

Sanctify them in the truth; Your word is
truth.

John 17:17 (NASB)

When you have a tough time forgiving yourself, do you wrestle with self-accusation and bitterness? How about self-condemnation? Self-criticism. Self-judgment. Self-hatred. Self-contempt. Self-rejection. Self-blame. Self-pity. Self-consciousness.

I don't know about you, but I've contended with them all.

Wrestling with Inner Lies

The carousel of seasons spun past, one year after another. As Ben grew, we tracked his development with milestone checklists on our pediatrician's chart. I was relieved to see that he kept up with his peers.

But residual muscle tension and facial tics tugged Ben's eyes and mouth to one side. He walked with an unsteady gait and dealt with frequent headaches. Inwardly, I cringed as I thought, "It's my fault that he's lost the ability to walk and talk normally. I can trace it back to his head injury from the car accident. I'm a terrible mom!"

Negative self-talk tormented me. I often prayed, "Jesus, I understand that You died to set me free. I feel anything but free!"

In my heart, I heard Him reply, "You're agreeing with the father of lies. But I defeated all his schemes on the cross. *All* of them. It's time to rid yourself of those angry thoughts and move forward with My truth."

"The message of the cross is foolish to those who are headed for destruction! But we who are being saved know it is the very power of God" (1 Corinthians 1:18 NLT). The great deceiver might try to feed us lies, but the Bible nourishes us with Jesus-truths—including the truth of who we *really* are. Jesus died on the cross for our sins. Along with salvation, we have the assurance of the Savior's power released in His act of redemption for us.

> *Self-criticism gets you nipping at your own tail. Round and round you go, until you become a thick blur. Grace whistles for you, grabs you by the paws, and pulls you to its chest.*

The enemy works overtime to destroy our identity. When he lies to us and says he has authority, we can weakly open our palms and let him have it. Or we can *let him have it!* With authority, we can stand with a foot on his neck and lift the sword of the Spirit, the Word of God. With deadly intent, we can strike swift and true.

Get Rid of the Lie. Exchange It for the Truth.

Here are a few lies from the accuser and truths to trade them out for:

Lie: I'm under condemnation.

Truth: I'm free from condemnation, because Christ is in me, and I'm in Him. *"Therefore there is now no condemnation for those who are in Christ Jesus"* (Romans 8:1).

Lie: I've committed the unforgivable sin.

Truth: It's *all* forgivable! It's *all* forgiven. I'm covered by the blood of Christ. *"But if we walk in the light, as he is in the light, we have fellowship with one another, and the blood of Jesus his Son cleanses us from all sin"* (1 John 1:7 ESV).

Lie: I'll never get it right!

Truth: Maybe I'm struggling, but Christ in me isn't. He empowers me! *"I can do all things through Christ who strengthens me"* (Philippians 4:13 NKJV).

> *I have no greater joy than to hear that my children are walking in the truth.*
> 3 John 1:4 ESV

Lie: I'm stuck. There's no way out.

Truth: He always provides a means of escape. *"No temptation has overtaken you but such as is common to man;*

and God is faithful, who will not allow you to be tempted beyond what you are able, but with the temptation will provide the way of escape also, so that you will be able to endure it" (1 Corinthians 10:13 NASB).

When we meditate on truth, our Redeemer shows us that our self-worth is not found in performance. Christ died for us, and we're redeemed apart from achievement. God loves us and accepts us, no matter how badly we've botched it.

Healing Joy

I love the craziness that Jesus brings to our homes. I kept a notebook of goofy things each of my kids said and did in their childhood. Here are a few from Ben's "funny book."

When Ben was two, he dropped a pink crayon into my iced tea when I wasn't looking. When I drained the glass, I spied the crayon and shrieked, "What's this?"

"Nyun-yun (crayon) tea," Ben replied, laughing.

He flicked the overhead light off and on while Tim was in the bathroom. He asked, "Do you like fireworks, Daddy?"

When he was four, Ben asked, "Mommy, do fire engines have bones? When I move, do my bones move? When I blink, do the bones in my eyes blink?"

"Mommy, I'm throwing away the fabric softener sheet. Will it soften the garbage?"

"Can I have four jobs when I grow up? I want to be a policeman, a clown, a baker, and a garage sale."

"I need to go to the police station to finish my last level of AWANA (Bible club). Daddy says he knows a way I can get a ride there for free!"

With each page of hilarity I wrote and later reread, I found myself relaxing. We had times when we struggled, all right. But buoyancy punctuated our days, too. And that's when He Who Tilts His Head Back with Hearty Laughter filled our home with healing joy.

Childhood Memories

Good-natured times flowed through my childhood, too. As an adult, over the years, I've sent my parents pages that have filled a notebook with vivid stories and images of fun family memories.

I revisited Sunday roast beef dinners and homemade iced tea and cookies. We six children played croquet and badminton in our backyard. A burbling creek there flowed past woods owned by a radio station. We walked New Jersey beaches, where we filled our lungs with the smell of salty sea air, our mouths with the taste of saltwater taffy and walnut-filled fudge from the boardwalk, and our ears with the sound of seagulls calling to one another as they dipped and rose above the edge of the piers.

Come rain or shine, for seven years, I pounded a newspaper route to deliver the *Evening Journal* to 50 customers in our suburban neighborhood in Delaware. I saved up my earnings, bought a piano, and took lessons. My mother, who taught me songs and rhymes for years, played duets with me from musicals like *The Sound of Music* and *Oklahoma!* My folks didn't miss one of my school concert choir performances.

My parents took us to church every week and taught us to pray. Sunday afternoons, my father and I pored over New

York Times crossword puzzles, snapping together the bits and pieces of our knowledge into spectacles that bore the lenses of two generations. Cousins, aunts, uncles, and grandparents joined us for holiday get-togethers and filled our home with laughter. Later, at family reunions, we fondly relived those memories.

Blame and Shame

Those were happy memories, for sure. Yet some days when I was growing up, we shifted into blame and shame mode. In the summer, flies buzzed through the house. Who let them in? In the winter, a door stood open to blustery winds and blizzards. Who let the heat out?

I got in trouble for dropping a bit of chocolate on a chair. I was called out for mistakes and grew flustered when I blew it. I began to think, "I don't want anyone to know I've made a mistake."

When I was 16, I went into the kitchen to make myself a peanut butter, jelly, and bologna sandwich. I reached for the bread drawer, but instead of sliding out like it had thousands of times before, it refused to open. I yanked hard. Suddenly, the handle snapped off in my hand. I bit my lip.

"Uh-oh. That wasn't supposed to happen," I thought. A short while later, my father called four of us children into the kitchen and asked who'd broken the bread drawer handle.

My brother and sisters spoke up.

"Not me."

"Not me."

"Not me."

"Not me," I echoed, swallowing hard, my heart

pounding. Inside, I secretly smacked a hand to my head. "Oh, great, now I'm a pathological liar." My dad was unhappy, and I didn't have the courage to own up to the crime until more than 30 years later at a family reunion—after reminding everyone that the statute of limitations was long past.

I've Got to Get It Right

As a kid, sometimes I was struck harshly for acting out, and my adrenals went crazy. My heart pounded. I felt trapped. With my boundaries busted, life felt beyond my control. I was super insecure.

I tried to play up my good points. I was a straight-A student. I joined Bible studies. I told my family that I wanted to become a nun after I graduated from high school.

Even so, blame and shame shadowed me.

Some days, my loud voice and laughter precipitated a cyclone of anger that picked me up and spun me around, leaving me dazed. I felt like Wile E. Coyote, with a cloud of dust rising around me and a ring of stars circling my head.

Mistakes' Consequences—Thunk!

Were my mistakes so outrageous, I wondered, that I deserved to be hurt when I made them? Sometimes when I blew it, though my father had good intentions, the intensity of his words and punishment left me in tears, feeling scared and wounded.

When my mistakes went by unnoticed, I was still wary of being found out later. Forget waiting for the other shoe to drop. I was convinced that I would someday open the closet of my failures, and the entire wardrobe would come crashing onto my head. Hats. Belts. Umbrellas. *Thunk! Thunk! Thunk! Ouch!*

That's when my perfectionism kicked into gear. I reasoned, "If I do things right, I can avoid getting hurt."

Where Are Those Boundaries When I Need Them?

Some days, I felt like I was missing the normal sense of stability I needed as a child. Fear was a formidable opponent to be reckoned with. I thought, "I'm not *causing* a problem. I *am* a problem." I internalized the pain and came to believe lies of the enemy.

I love books about boundaries. They reinforce a life lesson called Boundaries 101: a healthy boundary keeps the good in and the bad out. When I was hurt, my boundaries clearly hadn't protected me. My internal dialogue went crazy. I wasn't able to protect myself, let alone advocate for my own needs. That fueled internal anger, which then invited more falsehoods from the author of deceit.

Have you believed these lies like I once did? "I'm not wanted. I'm worthless. Everyone knows it." Or "I've got no voice in this situation. My opinion doesn't count."

Friend, you're Father God's precious child, and He loves you, no matter what you've done. And guess what? He loves you just as much on your worst day as He does on your best.

In *Broken Children, Grown-Up Pain,* Paul Hegstrom describes how childhood hurts can arrest our development:

"Many of us are dying inside because we can't see a past

wound as the source of our adult behaviors. We're powerless and helpless, feeling like children in an adult world. Our abilities to understand our emotions, resolve our conflicts, manage our anger, and cope with our sexuality were stolen from us when we were hurt. Because we're arrested in our development, we can't see the whole picture."[1]

The results of childhood trauma include guilt, shame and a skewed perspective. We lack trust; we fear truth; we doubt knowledge. At the point of trauma, the child instantly feels powerless and helpless. A chain reaction is set in motion: loss of self-respect, loss of sense of security, lack of trust, and fear of knowledge.[2]

A few years ago, I had an amazing talk with my father. He asked forgiveness for the harsh things he'd done. We talked it out and sorted through our issues. I forgave him and gave him a sincere hug. We found a new connectedness in the process. Today, we have a great relationship. I deeply love and admire him, and we now have an open relationship between us. I'm grateful for his willing heart, because God used that experience to bring me healing.

Reconciliation with parents is important, if and when God makes the call to take that step. To be set free from the wounds of a painful childhood, we need the knowledge and understanding of the purpose for which we were created.

Who We Are in Christ

What is our purpose? To walk in truth. Where is that found? In a GPS called the Bible.

If Jesus lives in your heart, you can say:

I am faithful (Ephesians 1:1).

I am God's child (John 1:12).

I have been justified (Romans 5:1).

I am Christ's friend (John 15:15).

I belong to God (1 Corinthians 6:20).

I am a member of Christ's Body (1 Corinthians 12:27).

I am assured all things work together for good (Romans 8:28).

I have been established, anointed, and sealed by God (2 Corinthians 1:21-22).

I am confident that God will perfect the work He has begun in me (Philippians 1:6).

See Appendix C for more Scriptures about our identity in Christ.

"For the law of the Spirit of life has set you free in Christ Jesus from the law of sin and death" (Romans 8:2 ESV). Because the Holy Spirit lives in you, you have the authority to release His empowerment in your circumstances and your mind. His life brings freedom so that you can let go of your past, accept yourself in the present, and get your head back in the game for the future.

Core Truth: When we exchange the accuser's lies for God-truths, we're empowered.

Let's Pray

Holy Spirit, as you lead me into truth, peel off layers of lies about my past, present, and future. You've spoken to me in the past. I have faith that You'll speak to me again in Your time. I'm covered by the blood of the Lamb. There is no condemnation for me, because I'm in Christ Jesus. Father, I am Your child, walking in Your truth, with great expectation that I'm bringing You joy.

Take the Next Step

Identify three of the deceiver's lies that you have believed about yourself. Write a God-truth and Bible verse to counter each one. Destroy the list of lies. Put the God-truths in your home, car, workplace, and on electronic apps to access in multiple places. Speak them aloud. What difference do you notice?

---

[1]Paul Hegstrom. *Broken Children, Grown-Up Pain: Understanding the Effects of Your Wounded Past*. Beacon Hill Press. 2006. p. 30.

[2]Ibid., 33-36.

Make Others' Promises Your Own

The lines have fallen to me in pleasant
places; Yes, I have a good inheritance.

Psalm 16:6 (NKJV)

A couple of years ago, on a flight from Oregon to Pennsylvania, I flipped open the airline magazine to its map and tracked our progress across the country. The map defined political borders, but peering through the window, I saw no such lines on the earth below. We traversed six of the Rocky Mountain states and 10 that spanned the Great Plains. But those expansive stretches of the earth beneath the aircraft were unmarked by manmade borders.

I used to see prayer in terms of territories. I saw dotted lines between myself and a person, business, or ministry that was receiving intercession. I thought that while they were cheered on and uplifted, those encouraging words didn't fall inside my borders.

How very unfair!

This One's for You

"You're entering a new season of growth and fruition," an intercessor prayed over a man at a Sunday evening prayer service. "You have the Lord's favor! Seeds you've been sowing for years have taken root. Make room for the increase."

At another prayer meeting, a speaker said to a couple, "You have a fantastic ability to hear the voice of the Holy Spirit."

Frowning, I wondered, "Why don't I get great promises like that?"

For years, I fought jealousy over prayers that spoke hope and expansion to others. I was certain the truths applied to them and maybe to a few others in the room, but they surely weren't meant for me.

Then, one day, in a church class, the facilitator said, "When prayer's happening, if a truth applies to you, appropriate it!" I raced home and looked up the definition of the word "appropriate." I found out that it means to take something for yourself. When a word of prayer or truth is spoken over someone, and the Holy Spirit says it belongs to you, it's yours!

Fireworks whistled, sang, and exploded in the sky overhead.

The Holy Spirit Taps My Shoulder

When the Holy Spirit got my attention and told me to start appropriating truths for myself, I felt a critical inner shift—probably one of the most meaningful changes in my faith walk.

I began to listen more carefully to prayers as they happened for other people. A speaker at church pointed to a woman near the back of the room and announced, "You are the Creator's treasure chest filled with jewels."

I whispered in my heart, "Holy Spirit, is that meant for me, too?"

I felt His gaze on me. My insides warmed. He whispered back with a soft smile, "Yes."

At another meeting, a prayer leader told a woman, "Doors are opening for you. Walk right through them with confidence."

And another: "He's not hiding things *from* you. He's hiding them *for* you!"

I asked the Holy Spirit if He saw me like that. He nodded.

A well-known minister spoke to a prayer warrior and told her, "God is dispatching angels to help you battle the injustice in your situation. You'll get protection and messages from heavenly hosts!"

In my heart, I asked the Holy Spirit, "Are there angels for me, too?" I had the sense that He was confirming their presence.

I wondered if this "appropriating" stuff was too good to be true.

The Adversary Says You're Not Good Enough

One day, a fellow member of a team praying for a business owner said to him, "When you forgive some business associates, you'll see your company grow." Immediately, I thought of a man I needed to forgive. I wondered if I might appropriate that business expansion for the software company my husband and I own.

But a thought came to me: "Look how long I've

harbored a grudge. My attitude towards that man rules me out. No way could that breakthrough possibly be for me."

I stopped to evaluate those words. Was I disqualified? When God assured me that I was not, I recognized the lies as a distraction from the adversary. Then, I heard the Holy Spirit say in my heart, "Forget imaginary standards! That promise is for you, too. A forgiving heart is just what you need for success in your business. Forgive that man."

So, mid-meeting, I battled the prince of darkness by whispering under my breath, "Therefore, there is now no condemnation for those who are in Christ Jesus.

"And that word does, too, belong to me. The Holy Spirit says so!"

I released the man from judgment and simply forgave him. Then I moved forward with eager expectation that with newfound grace, our business would take off. Did that happen immediately? No. But reviewing my promises regularly allowed forgiveness to remain in my spirit so that my level of expectancy would remain fresh. And I gained all that ground from a promise offered in prayer for someone else!

Sometimes, I felt I heard Father God say, "That belongs to you. Take it!" Other times, it seemed He said, "No, My child. That's for just them this time." But when He said no, it didn't bother me, because as I grow in accepting His deep love for me, I'm learning that each of us has our own Kingdom assignment and different plans to go with them.

It's like that for you, too. You have a unique purpose in the fold. Jesus calls Himself the Gate. You can come in and go out and find pasture. In the process, accept His love for you. *"And I pray that you, being rooted and established in love, may have power, together with all the Lord's holy people, to grasp how wide and long and high and deep is the love of Christ, and to know this love that surpasses knowledge"* (Ephesians 3:17–19).

Which Bible Verses Apply to You?

About now, you might be thinking, "When I hear someone pray, which Bible verses apply to me?" Friend, *all* the promises in the Bible belong to you. It doesn't matter who's being prayed for. The Good Book is yours, beginning to end.

> **The Redeemer's promises are not just true. They're true for you.**

And when He Who Accepts Like No Other releases forgiveness over others in the room, accept the truth for yourself. Absorb the words. Make them your own. Forgiveness. Favor. Healing. Increase in finances. Restoration for your family. Advancement on the job. Next time a prayer is spoken over an individual or group, try it. Ask the Holy Spirit, "Is this for me, too?"

Does a truth resonate in your soul? Appropriate it!

Core Truth: Promises spoken over others are sometimes God's way of speaking to us.

Let's Pray

Father God, on the worst days, what the enemy meant to confine, You're using for explosive expansion to accomplish

Your purposes in my life. Holy Spirit, quicken to my heart which promises spoken over others also belong to me.

I give You permission to strip off any preconceived boundaries I've imagined and I open my spirit to the flow of Your truth. As I take in Your Scripture, I give it room to resonate inside me and to release fresh waves of self-acceptance.

Take the Next Step

The next time you hear someone being prayed for, ask the Holy Spirit, "Is this for me?" Appropriate the promises that belong to you. Jot down any words, images, and Scriptures that go with them.

God Already Paid for That!

He did this once for all when he offered up himself.

Hebrews 7:27 (ESV)

I love entering into Jesus-joy with young children. A few years back, I poured my creative juices into a weeklong summer program for kids supervised by several enthusiastic teens and adults. We worshiped with sign language. We performed funny puppet shows. We snapped together jigsaw puzzle pieces with key words and Scripture verses and formed the image of a lighthouse beside a harbor. The kids made crafts and scampered across the grass in the sun.

By the end of the program that Friday, the staff had worked up a big appetite. After packing up materials, I arrived at the buffet-style cafeteria ahead of the others and paid for their lunches. When they arrived, they filled their plates, reached the last counter, and took out their wallets to pay. The cashier smiled and shook her head. She told them it was already taken care of.

It's the same way with our sins. Once we repent, we encounter our Father's forgiveness through the sacrifice of His Son, Jesus Christ. Trying to offset iniquity with good works might seem like a good idea. But who needs to pay twice? Jesus has already picked up the tab. When we acknowledge that we have been given the gift of His life, we freely receive our redemption.

The Power of Believing Together

When we find something especially difficult, we need to remember that grace is freely given. I've often struggled to let down my defenses and tell people when I'm hurting. When my finances were skimpy, I rarely told anyone. When my body throbbed with cycles of fibromyalgia and I got very little sleep, I didn't ask for prayer, embarrassed that I might be judged for ongoing chronic illness. When I had brain fog and post-traumatic stress disorder following the car accident, it was hard to know which way to turn. I wondered why, while others were getting healed, the fibromyalgia continued to trouble me.

What I needed most was for fellow believers to agree with what Jesus had already accomplished on the cross and to declare it with me. I didn't need another book, list of "to do's," or a script of precise words to say. I needed to know that I satisfied the Lord just by being His kid. I wanted the assurance that God accepted me unconditionally. I needed His invisible world: one that held strength and healing.

Slowly, gradually, I found that His world was, in fact, visible. He whispered, "Where you find Me, you'll find home." When we trust our Savior's plan for releasing sin, our confidence can rise, because we know that there's nothing that can separate us from His love.

He sometimes allows us to go through circumstances so that we can perceive His love for us, deep, deep down in the core of our being. One of the amazing gifts in the process is learning the truth that He never wastes pain. *Never.*

> *That you should dare to heal yourself by this simple act is a signal to the world that God's love is a power within you.*[1]
> *~ Lewis Smedes*

So put away your cash. Jesus is putting His wallet back into His overalls pocket. This one's on Him.

Core Truth: Since Jesus paid the price, we don't have to.

Let's Pray

Father, increase my trust that Your plan has already been accomplished on the cross. Thank You, Jesus, for reconciling the world to Yourself, not counting my trespasses against me, and entrusting to me the message of reconciliation (2 Corinthians 5:19).

By Your blood, You entered into the holy place, having obtained eternal redemption for me (Hebrews 9:12). There is nothing I can do or say that will make You love me more or less than You do at this very moment. Thank You for this deep love.

Take the Next Step

Draw a cross. Add a symbol or picture that stands for what was redeemed for you there, such as fear, shame, sin, resentment, or lost time. Above the cross, write "Paid. Forgiven."

---

[1]Lewis Smedes. *Forgive and Forget: Healing the Hurts We Don't Deserve.* HarperOne. 2007. p. 77

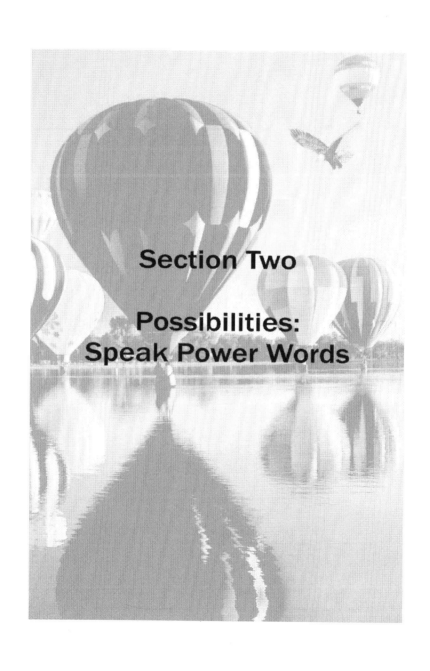

Section Two

Possibilities:
Speak Power Words

Change Your Brain Patterns

We are destroying speculations and every
lofty thing raised up against the knowledge
of God, and we are taking every thought
captive to the obedience of Christ.

2 Corinthians 10:5 (NASB)

In order to excel at warfare with the enemy, the prince of this world, you and I need to be prepared for battle every day. Where does that fight happen? In our minds. Our primary weapon is our thoughts, which are powerful—for better or for worse. When our thoughts and emotions are filled with stress, anxiety, fear, anger, or resentment, the mind-body connection affects our physical health.

Have you experienced physical symptoms when you were upset with yourself? What were they like?

The Mind-Emotion-Spirit Connection

Dr. Caroline Leaf, a cognitive neuroscientist who specializes in neuropsychology, is one of my favorite authors. Her work explores the interconnectedness between our minds, emotions, and spirits. She is an expert on brain science and explains how it works together with the truth of Scripture. She teaches about neuroplasticity, the ability for changes in thinking to affect the brain and bring about behavioral changes.

Dr. Leaf reports, "75 to 95 percent of the illnesses that plague us today are a direct result of our thought life. What we think about affects us physically and emotionally. It's an epidemic of toxic emotions."[1] She explains that medical research increasingly indicates that consciously controlling our thought lives is one of the best ways—if not *the* best way— to detoxify the brain.

Old Patterns of Toxic Thoughts

Negative thoughts create an environment in our brains that makes it hard for anything positive to happen. In her book, *Switch on Your Brain*, Dr. Leaf reports that unforgiveness and resentment are toxic thoughts. New, healthy thoughts, such as forgiveness, are like tiny new plants that need to grow. But shifting gears doesn't happen automatically, especially if we have carried a thought pattern for years. Once we've gotten rid of toxic thoughts, it's possible that our minds will shift back and try to regrow them.[3]

> Get rid of those toxic thoughts and emotions that can consume and control your mind. Change in your thinking is essential to detox the brain.[2]
> ~ Caroline Leaf

From a Toxic Waste Site to a Green Garden

How can we convert a mind that has become a dumping ground for negativity into a place that grows more productive thoughts? Dr. Leaf says that the secret is thinking healthy thoughts. If we consistently produce positive thoughts for three cycles of 21 days, they will become automatic.

The healthy brain's thoughts are proteins that look like a tree with leaf-filled branches. When they're seven days old, the connections where the branches grow have little bumps called spines. After 14 days, they look like lollipops. After 21 days, they look like mushrooms. Our thoughts become stronger. This is true for positive and negative thoughts.[4]

What's happening? When the brain connections look like mushrooms, the proteins have changed to become self-sustaining, like those in long-term memory. We have created new thought patterns. But we still need healthy new thoughts to keep the pattern alive.

Whenever we revert back to a toxic thought, such as resentment or bitterness, the process is reversed. It breaks down the healthy thought and rebuilds the toxic one. We can ensure our thoughts are healthy only when we have them under our conscious control: when we take every thought captive.

You and I can make strong new memories by taking charge of our minds. When we replace a negative thought with a positive one, we're making important neurotransmitters flow. These chemical messengers in the brain carry electrical impulses, transmitting signals from one neuron to another. In the presence of this improved brain chemistry, deep changes occur in our brain cells. That's good news when it comes to the healthy thoughts we need in order to forgive ourselves.

We can keep the following key truths in mind as we work to detoxify our brains and create a healthy environment within.

Resentment is a toxic thought that can be released and replaced with healthy thoughts of self-forgiveness. We can ask our Helper to enter the process of relinquishing negative thoughts. When we forgive ourselves, we make our brains smarter!

Our minds can physically change our brains. When we concentrate on healthy thoughts of gratitude, strength, and purpose, our brains change. To a neuroscientist, new brain activity has the physical appearance of fresh green leaves sprouting on a tree. Remember, we have the mind of Christ! (See 1 Corinthians 2:16.) We can ask the Holy Spirit to "rewire" our thoughts. Every day, we can pray, "Holy Spirit, as I reach ahead, I'm aligning my thoughts with Yours."

Proteins in the brain can make new thoughts automatic and self-sustaining. When we gain and use new thoughts for 21-day cycles, our brains can get rewired. Neurons that fire together wire together. Reading or listening to Scripture is similar to syncing a phone app with a computer: it connects us to the power of God's Spirit. Out of that flow, we can think and speak from an identity birthed out of communion with Him.

Bring into captivity every thought. Practice. Practice some more. New thought patterns become automatic after three weeks, but we need to remind ourselves again and again in order to avoid lapsing back into old patterns. Negatives creep in without invitation. Negativity will grow if fed. We need to speak out God-truths from His Word, journal them, and make a conscious effort to stick with His forgiving flow to coax our brains back into a positive place.

Laughter brings life to your brain. Memories of Ben's childhood still make me chuckle. He was a high-energy kid who needed reminders about his bedtime routine to keep him on track. When Ben was four, I reminded him, "After your bath, first thing, you should put on your pajamas. It's always the same."

Ben joked, "I will keep that in my mind. If it pops out, I will put it back in!"

When he was six, Ben filled out a page asking for his city, state, continent, and planet. He said, "What's my planet? Earth! So what do they think, I live on Neptune or something?"

Where intentional thinking and speaking go, actions follow. When we forgive ourselves, we can work, play, and relate to others more easily and joyfully. Thinking new thoughts will also help us view life differently. Even if our circumstances are not perfect, we can practice gratitude and forgiveness, and that will change how we experience life.

Every summer, my kids had new chores to do around the house. One June morning, I told Ben that his responsibilities included helping with yardwork. With a twinkle in his eye, he said, "Mom, 'summer job' is an oxymoron!"

The Devil Speaks in the First Person

I've learned that the prince of darkness plays dirty. When we engage in battle with the devil, he usually doesn't say, "Look what *you* did. *You're* a failure." No, he usually sneaks into our heads and uses the first person. He says, "Look what *I* did. *I'm* a complete failure." He makes it sound like we're saying that to ourselves. When we agree, we partner with him. That's when we need to slow down and test each thought to see if it's based in truth.

We can do this by checking in with the Word and with the Lord. We can find out where we're out of alignment and where we're stuck. And then we do heart checks. He'll show us the next steps, and if we give Him permission, He'll show us the root of the issue and cleanse the source of hindrances.

Flowing-Water Forgiveness Checks

Some days, my mind feels like a brown, brackish pond with thick clouds of mosquitoes buzzing overhead. So I go for a walk. When I see flowing water—like a stream, river, or fountain—I pause and ask the Lord, "Who do I need to forgive?"

Jesus brings people to mind. I release judgment and take a couple of minutes to forgive them. Sometimes He tells me I need to forgive myself. I scoop up a twig or leaf, and imagine it's my negative thoughts. I drop it into the currents that tumble over rocks and swish through dappled patches of clear water. Soon it's out of sight.

"Lord," I say in my heart, "I can't see it anymore."

He replies, "Neither can I."

"As far as the east is from the west, so far has He removed our transgressions from us" (Psalm 103:12 NASB). I love that Jesus sweeps our sins away in opposite directions! How far is the east from the west? An infinite distance that goes on forever.

Focus on Fresh Holy Spirit Neuroconnections

You can give the Holy Spirit permission to transform your mind. Picture the neuropathways in your head like a superhighway, ribbon upon ribbon, with millions of intertwining freeways. At the sites where they intersect, invite the Holy Spirit to release His thoughts. At the bramble hedges in memories where self-directed points of anger begin, we can command the process to stop. Envision bursts of Holy Spirit light displacing the bramble hedges.

Picture vibrant, green-leaf-bearing trees and hearts—fresh, healthy thought patterns with positive affirmations:

- *I'm bright.*
- *I'm successful.*
- *I'm creative.*
- *I can think of a new way of doing this that will make it better.*
- *My future holds promise.*
- *I'm grateful for the transitions I have no control over, because they're propelling me into fresh ways of seeing and doing things.*

Soon, your internal dialogue will say, "I'm at peace with that memory. I'm at peace with myself."

A Sacred Internal Duet

I often go into worship mode, no matter where I am. I might be in a business meeting, processing emails, or on the phone with a friend. I select a song from a bank of audio files I've preloaded in my brain. I bring up the lyrics on the monitor of my mind and enter into Jesus' flow as I sing in my head. I imagine Jesus singing with me, as we trade the melody and harmony back and forth.

When I do, I feel the shift. My spirit rises. The tangible, realized presence of Jesus is in that moment.

His power never changes. Our perception of His power may change from one moment to the next, but it is, in fact, unchanging.

Take Back the Driver's Seat in Your Brain

One day, as I was praying, I had a vision. I saw myself in the back of a service van that picked up and delivered linen to medical buildings. On the route, as we stopped again and again, the driver ruthlessly piled one wet towel after another on top of me. For hours, I felt cramped, crushed, and smothered, trying to shift filthy washcloths and sheets around me in an attempt to get comfortable.

My annoyance grew as I looked at the scowling driver. He tossed a smelly towel into the back of the van, and it smacked me in the back of the head. Enough was enough! I shoved the dirty linen away, rose up, and charged him. I grabbed him by the collar, and threw him to the curb.

"This is my van," I said, forcefully, "Get out!" I dumped the ratty old linens and climbed behind the steering wheel with Jesus on the seat beside me, on a mission to fill the van with clean white replacements.

It's like that when you and I war for control of our minds and hearts. We need to take back what's rightfully ours—every thought! But don't imagine for a minute that the battle ends once the enemy is ejected from the driver's seat. We're likely to find him trying to return again and again.

I asked the Holy Spirit, "How do I maintain my sense of authority?"

He responded, "I'm your GPS. Let's go!"

You don't have to go it alone. If you feel like you need to improve your thought life, ask Him to reveal areas where you need change and to give you the desire and energy to commit to that change. Find counselors, mentors, prayer partners, and other friends to help you live up to that commitment and take back what is yours.

When we understand the process of how our minds can change our brains, we create positive thoughts that flow with God-truths. Self-acceptance is the net result.

Core Truth: The Holy Spirit rewires our minds with His thoughts.

Let's Pray

Lord, I praise You because as I think within myself, so am I (Proverbs 23:7). I let go of any negative thoughts about myself and purpose to focus on positive, healthy ones. I bring into captivity every thought, and I make it obedient to You. I'm not conforming to the pattern of this world but am transformed by the renewing of my mind (Romans 12:2). Thank You for renewing and ordering my thoughts.

Because You live in me, Your thoughts are mine—creative, flowing and connected. Pour through my neuropathways. Rewire my thoughts with Your Word, which says that I am forgiven, cleansed, and free. From this point forward, I have a renewed, reclaimed mind.

Take the Next Step

With colored pencils, draw a tree with scrawny, thorny branches. Identify and label the branches with names of negative thoughts that need to be eliminated in your brain—such as guilt, anger, resentment, envy, or fear. Draw a second tree and give it big, green, leafy branches. What healthy, growing thoughts are springing up? Label them.

Ask the Holy Spirit to illuminate which thought patterns He wants to remove and which He wants to grow. Using colored pencils or markers, label three branches with positive thought patterns and align your thoughts with them for the next 21 days. Share the results with a friend.

---

[1]Dr. Caroline Leaf. *Controlling Your Toxic Thoughts.* http://drleaf.com/about/toxic-thoughts. (Retrieved September 29, 2016.)

[2]Ibid.

[3]Dr. Caroline Leaf. *Switch on Your Brain: The Key to Peak Happiness, Thinking, and Health.* Baker Books. 2013. p. 152.

[4]Ibid., p. 153.

New Dialogues with Yourself

Be kind to one another, tenderhearted,
forgiving one another, as God in Christ
forgave you.

Ephesians 4:32 (ESV)

Jesus loves us and calls us to be kind not only to others, but to *ourselves*—just as tenderhearted, just as forgiving, just as loving. And that includes self-talk.

In your running conversations with yourself, are you encouraging? Or is your dialogue filled with constant criticism? What you think will steer what you say. Your internal words release energy that affects your circumstances.

"The tongue has the power of life and death, and those who love it will eat its fruit" (Proverbs 18:21). What we say has the ability to release life in the spirit realm. That means every word we utter—or even think—is giving life to something. What are we giving life to?

Most of my life, I talked harshly to myself. To be honest, I continue to rely on the Holy Spirit to help me change my internal dialogue every day. "Lord," I pray, "show me how to speak to myself as nicely as I talk to my friends!"

The Whole World Can See My Mistake

Before I knew it, Ben's preschool years were over, and it was time for kindergarten. With a twinkle in his deep blue eyes, he announced, "Mom, I want a haircut!"

"Okay, Ben," I frowned. "I'll make an appointment." But I knew what was coming.

As he climbed onto a chair at the children's hair salon, I thought, "Another trim, another chance for the whole world to see the huge scar on his head."

Snip, snip went the hairdresser's scissors. I slouched down and hid behind a magazine in the waiting area. She held up her scissors and asked, "How do you like the cut?"

The deep, pronounced incision arching over his right ear seemed to shout, "Look, everyone! Head injury! Mom's fault!"

I swallowed hard. "That's fine," I mumbled. I paid, yanked Ben's arm, and we fled to the car. My heart raced.

Once behind the wheel, I said to myself, "Why do I overreact like this every time Ben gets a haircut? Probably because everyone sees how stupid I am. Worse, I should have gotten over this years ago. I'm an immature Christian, dwelling on the accident like this!"

When Anger Speaks Louder Than Love

"Lord," I vowed. "I'm so thankful You healed Ben! You've given me a second chance. I'll never lose my temper with him."

Like every other kid on the block, Ben, along with Andy

and Emily, left muddy footprints on the rug, dried chunks of Play-Doh on the couch, and toys in unlikely corners of the house. Sometimes, I found myself roaring at Ben for tearing pages in books or refusing to eat his vegetables.

One night, six-year-old Ben stalled for what seemed like hours past his bedtime. After he took a bath, he put on his PJs and ran, squealing, down the hallway. I'd had a long day. Rubbing the back of my neck, I bent over the bathtub and retrieved toys he'd left behind. I stepped into the living room. Cookie crumbs were scattered across a rug I'd vacuumed just minutes before. A headache came out of nowhere. Something inside me snapped.

I roared at Ben and sent him to his room. *Slam!* went the door. *Bam! w*ent my escalating anger. Immediately, I thought, "What just happened?"

"I'm mad at Ben. But I'm even madder at myself. He's just a kid who wants to avoid bedtime. Like all boys, he runs. He leaves crumbs. Can't you see that yelling at him shows a hopelessly hard heart?" Now I was "doing doubles"—angry with myself for being angry.

I wanted to be happy. I craved kind, pleasant conversations with myself. I needed to reframe my self-talk. It seemed that I could speak kindly to other people most of the time but was harsh and relentless with myself.

I asked my Comforter and Counselor, the Holy Spirit, how I could change. He showed me that we need to shift expectations of ourselves so that we're open to changes He wants to make in us to mature us. When that happens, we're primed for better self-talk.

Tips to Improve Your Inner Dialogue

Keep regular devotional times, even when you're struggling. On days when I skip my quiet time, I'm out of step with the Holy Spirit. But on days when I make time for Him, I get into sync with His thoughts. *"If we live by the Spirit, let us also walk by the Spirit"* (Galatians 5:25 NASB). Journal each quiet time, even if the entry is short. Trust that He is still in those times.

When you're stressed or exhausted, take time to care for yourself. I'm a writer, and I love words. But I struggle to focus when I'm on overload. Do you find that, too? Give yourself a break and shift into stress-reduction mode. Get a massage. Listen to your favorite music, eat fruit salad, drink extra water, or go for a walk to clear your head. The words that follow are likely to be simpler, softer, and more accepting.

Believe that the sovereign Lord is about to shift things in your favor. Fill your mind and self-talk with hope from heaven about your future. *"Therefore I tell you, whatever you ask in prayer, believe that you have received it, and it will be yours"* (Mark 11:24 ESV). Sure, doubt might temporarily distract us from Christ-certainties, but Jesus is our primary focus. He's got things under control. God is always good; sometimes, like a radar using radio waves to detect aircraft, we need to make "sweeps" for His goodness.

Ask the Holy Spirit for *His* words and allow them to permeate your self-talk. *"Call upon me and come and pray to me, and I will hear you"* (Jeremiah 29:12 ESV). I often ask the Holy Spirit, "What are You feeling? What are You saying?" I listen carefully and then whisper those words to myself throughout the day. Sometimes, I hear just one word, like "trust" or "angels," and text it to Tim. He texts back, "We just laugh at the enemy. He cannot succeed." There is nothing like a spontaneous and uplifting word from the Holy Spirit.

Take note of encouraging words used by mentors and other friends. Keep a word bank of affirmations and expressions. When a phrase catches my attention, I add it to an app that can be accessed from several devices.

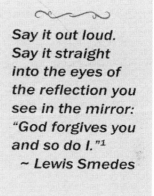

Say it out loud. Say it straight into the eyes of the reflection you see in the mirror: "God forgives you and so do I."[1]
~ Lewis Smedes

Three Quick Secrets to Success

1. **Instead of calling a situation a "problem," call it a "challenge"** so that your mind frames it in terms of a positive invitation to grow.

2. **For every negative comment you say to yourself, say five positive things:** "I might have blown it, but here are five things I got right."

3. **Speak to yourself as if you were a close friend.**

Give yourself some good-natured grace. You'll be glad you did.

Remember Your Royal Roots

When dealing with an especially painful failure, say, "Though this has been tough, I'm letting it go. I'm a unique, wonderful kid of the Lord Most High, the great King. He loves me no matter what!" We're Kingdom dwellers. We need to practice our royalty when we get frustrated. What does a queen say to herself when she quickly dashes off an email with misinformation? When she's too tired to spend time talking to the King? When she calls someone by the wrong name? She doesn't beat herself up. Out of her wealth and royalty, she evokes her sense of privilege and authority and lets it go. She moves on so that she can focus on Kingdom business.

> God has budgeted for our failure. Our failure cannot diminish the Kingdom, therefore it cannot diminish us.[2]
>
> ~ Graham Cooke

When you feel like giving up, say, "I'm taking this one step at a time. I'm right behind You, Lord." With infusions of His peace, we're freshly connected with Him, and new conversations with ourselves flow as His affirmations become ours.

Friend, many God-affirmations return to us when we lift sincere praise to Him in worship. We become one with Him. His presence is a safe place. When His thoughts are ours, what we say to ourselves will reflect what He thinks and says, and we can walk forward in the confidence found in His Spirit.

Core Truth: When we're in step with the Holy Spirit, we speak to ourselves with a renewed soul.

Let's Pray

Father, I commit to spend regular time alone with You. Fill my workplace, neighborhood, and home with Your thoughts. Jesus, I'm open to new expressions of Your affirmation. Holy Spirit, I'm listening for new words as You reveal them to me. I make them my own.

Take the Next Step

Write three Holy Spirit affirmations and speak them aloud. You might want to begin with these:

- *"I'm speaking the truth in love to myself and maturing spiritually into Christ"* (Ephesians 4:15).

- *"I'm speaking to myself with encouragement, because my heart and mind are protected with His peace"* (Philippians 4:7).

- *"I'm persevering in uplifting self-talk and gaining confidence that will be richly rewarded"* (Hebrews 10:35, 36).

---

[1]Lewis Smedes. *The Art of Forgiving.* Ballantine Books. 1997. p. 102.

[2]Graham Cooke. *Making the Most of Failure.*
http://www.elijahlist.com/words/display_word/2207. (Retrieved September 29, 2016.)

The Science of
Event-Changing Thoughts

*God . . . gives life to the dead and calls into
being that which does not exist.*

Romans 4:17 (NASB)

Most of my life, I haven't been much of a Bill Nye the Science Guy. As a student, I got through Chemistry and Physics by memorizing vocabulary. With a decent photographic memory, I retrieved charts and diagrams from mental "snapshots" of textbook pages. But my system broke down when application questions required a working knowledge of cause and effect. I could define "hydrogen" and "oxygen" but had no clue how the molecules teamed up to make water, steam, and ice.

Years later, I heard about a science called quantum physics. The more I learned, the more excited I grew. I thought, "Now here's a fun science I never knew existed."

I learned scientific principles of our world, including those in quantum physics, from an intriguing book called *Awaken the Sleeper* by Dr. Nick Castellano. I've become a huge fan. From him, I learned that everything is composed of energy, and energy pulses in waves. Dr. Castellano reports these facts about how the physics principles work:

- **Thoughts attract things.** A thought firmly fixed in your mind will attract the things represented by that thought. Thus, if you think negative thoughts, you will attract negative events, people, and circumstances and reinforce your negative thoughts. If you focus on peace, love, and joy, you will attract people, things, and situations that reinforce your state of peace, love, and joy.

- **Words focus thought.** Words are more powerful than thoughts. The word is a focused thought. A word is like light focused into a laser. It has power to create. Words have great energy and energy affects matter since all matter is energy. What you speak in faith over and over, you create. Are your words about good, positive things or fearful, negative things?

- **Energy determines speed.** What you focus on and believe and the amount of positive or negative energy you put around that event will dictate what and how quickly it is pulled from the unseen (invisible) to the seen (visible). Quantum physics calls this "collapsing the quiff."

> What we believe in our heart we receive in our world.[1]
> ~ Dr. Nick Castellano

- **Action is still important.** If you focus on a positive outcome in an environment of love, joy and peace (the Kingdom environment) and your focus is performed in hope (assurance that it will be done), and this is followed by the action step of faith (acting and feeling as if it were already done), you will collapse ["pop"] the quiff and bring the unseen event into the seen.

- **Walk, talk, and act as if your desire were already done.** Don't worry about how it will be done. That's God's job. Focus on seeing yourself in the done, finished, completed place. Relax—and create an environment of peace. Recognize that God exists and is in everything.[2]

In effect, quantum physics is all about moving things from possibility to actuality by expecting and speaking.

The Quantum Reality of it All

In Dr. Caroline Leaf's book, *How to Switch on Your Brain*, she outlines the main principles of quantum physics.

- "Our perceptions determine the outcome; we perceive the world through the thoughts (memories) we have built into our brains."

- "Particles move backward and forward in time and appear in all possible places at once."

I believe God is taking us through the material world into the spiritual world to get to know him more deeply, and the quantum concept is part of this journey.[3]
~ Dr. Caroline Leaf

- "The observer determines the direction in which the possibilities may collapse. In the quantum universe, as we—the observers—affect phenomena, space, and time, we turn possibilities into realities. Mind changes matter."

- "The random and unpredictable nature of quantum physics is a way God shows us that we do not control the future. He does."[4]

Personal Transformation, One Thought at a Time

Dr. Gayle Rogers' book, *The Whole Soul: Rescripting Your Life for Personal Transformation*, is one of the best resources for changing debilitating thoughts and mindsets with God's Word. She describes key life-changing transformation guidelines.

Dr. Rogers says, "As your mind is opened to the reality of the power and potential humans possess, you will begin to function at a different level. If humankind can only grasp the power of our thinking mechanisms, both from a scientific and spiritual perspective, we can do so much more in life. As we become more accountable to ourselves and others by taking responsibility of what is allowed to ruminate in our mind, we will experience life at a higher level. We must understand that every event, every circumstance occurring in our lives, is the

> *Think about exploring the capacity and strength of your mind and what it is capable of doing with you giving it instructions.*[5]
> ~ Dr. Gayle Rogers

78

direct result of either our thoughts, or we become the recipient of somebody else's thoughts."[6]

I was fascinated to find out that when we expect something to happen, matter is changed at the subatomic level. I know that sounds kind of crazy, but it's true.

That meant good news: I could get rid of all the garbage thoughts I'd lived with most of my life—like I was a rotten daughter, mom, or wife. I wore myself out, obsessing that I had missed a dream job as a full-time teacher—or maybe it had missed me. I felt like I deserved to lose. Negativity was such a habit for me that even if people didn't say anything negative, I made things up myself.

I was hounded by self-condemnation and self-resentment. I needed to get rid of old ways of thinking and to turn on new ways of thinking.

What you and I say alters the course of events about to happen. If we say, "There's no way that's going to work out—the track record says *that's* impossible," then we can expect a failed outcome. But when we say, "I declare and decree that this is easy—it's going to be wildly successful!" we actually speak a positive effect into existence.

Imagine the possibilities!

When Attraction Meets Prayer

Once I caught on to quantum physics, I got swept up into what the God of Many Dimensions was releasing as I was expecting, praying, and speaking. I saw for the first time that at the physics level our expectations *activate* things in the natural. The words we use are critical.

I used to believe about 15 percent of the affirmations I

spoke aloud. I shrugged off the other 85 percent as a loss. I thought, "Speaking out expectations and seeing them happen works for everyone but me." But then I practiced with friends, and we cheered one another on. Weeks later, I believed about 50 percent of what I said. Then slowly, after several months, I felt a shift. I believed 85 to 90 percent of the words I spoke and soon 95 percent! Declaring and decreeing results actually brought them about.

Most of my life, I've had a tough time removing lids from water bottles. Without realizing it, I frowned and concentrated on the "closedness" of the container. "Here's another one," I thought, "just as impossibly tight as the last." But then I recognized an old thought pattern and realized that I could consciously decide whether the task was hard. One night, over dinner, I simply changed my focus to the "openness" of the lid. "This is easy," I thought, envisioning the cap twisting readily under my fingers. The lid came right off! From then on, opening water bottles was a breeze.

When I got hold of that, I prayed over anything and everything! It seemed like quiff-popping could strip the paint off a wall.

I've prayed one-on-one with thousands of people. Sometimes I prayed, "The illness in your body is gone. Jesus has completely healed you." I told many that they were in the right place at the right time and that God was using their circumstances to bring encouragement to others. I told others that their marriages were strong, and a new understanding of their spouses would change their homes. I spoke to strengths in businesses and laughed out loud, celebrating rapid growth for corporate teams. The words and laughter were like magnets, drawing the steel filings of positive results into alignment with Christ's supernatural power.

People sometimes returned later and told me about physical healing. Others told me that when they encouraged their families, joy blossomed. We saw hope restored to marriages. We celebrated businesses' expansion. I was excited that so many drew close to God in the process. Of course, there were plenty of times when I didn't get to hear the outcomes, but I trusted in faith that breakthrough was activated.

What we think and say has a very real influence on the course of events.

What words are you using? What effect do they have right now on your current circumstances? What might they change for your future?

Core Truth: Our thoughts can activate and change the course of events.

Let's Pray

Father of Possibilities, I choose positive thoughts and actions and fully expect wonderful things to unfold. I pull things from possibility into actuality simply by expecting and speaking them into existence. I'm changing my words to line up with Your Word. I'm speaking the power of relentless belief in Your unshakable power.

Take the Next Step

List three wishes. Get specific and include details. Where will you go? What changes will happen? Then ask the Holy Spirit for His vision of success and record it. Leave a blank page in your journal for Him to write on in the future.

Envision and speak out positive outcomes. Tell friends what God is revealing. Notice what happens in your expectancy. Be open to Holy Spirit possibilities!

[1] Dr. Nick Castellano. *Awaken the Sleeper:* Uhios Publishing. 2010. p. 34.

[2] Ibid., pp. 23-47.

[3] Dr. Caroline Leaf. *Switch on Your Brain: The Key to Peak Happiness, Thinking, and Health.* Baker Books. 2013. p. 122.

[4] Ibid., pp. 105, 120-122.

[5] Dr. Gayle Rogers. *The Whole Soul: Rescripting Your Life for Personal Transformation.* Kingdom House Publishing. 2014. p. 70.

[6] Ibid., p. 56.

Change the Atmosphere: Speak Truth Out Loud

You will also decree a thing, and it will be established for you; and light will shine on your ways.

Job 22:28 (NASB)

Playing miniature golf at a resort in central Oregon with Tim, I shaded my eyes with my hand, looking at the double-backed twisty loop that lay ahead. I frowned. "Now here's a tough one," I said. I tapped the ball, and six strokes later it dropped into the hole.

"Hey," I said, tilting my head. "I think I can do better."

Tim asked, "What are you going to do?"

I replied, "I'm going to change what I say before I tee off."

I stepped to the next hole and announced, "This one is going right in. Watch this—a hole in one!" I swung at the ball. It sprang to life, scooted down the mini-fairway and immediately sank into the hole. I did a double take.

Then I jumped up and down, pumping the golf club over my head. "Wow!" I exclaimed. "Did you see that? It went right in."

Tim grinned. "Hey! Can you do that again?"

"Maybe. Let's check it out."

I conducted a fun little experiment. For three of the next holes, I said, "This looks hard. I don't know if I can do it." Each hole took six or seven strokes.

Before I swung the club for the next one, I smiled and announced, "Here's a hole in one!" The ball went directly into the cup. My eyebrows shot up. And then it happened again!

Just as we gain a surge of strength from others' prayers and words of encouragement, we activate the Mighty One's power in us when we speak truths aloud for ourselves. This is one of the best ways to create an atmosphere of self-acceptance.

The Holy Spirit reveals words of encouragement. We can declare His God-truths in the kitchen, in the car, at the mall, at the post office, on a nature walk—anytime or anywhere. When we're in conflict with a difficult person, we can dissolve negative emotions by speaking God-truths softly. Releasing His power in the middle of stressful, worrisome, or fearful situations dismisses the false authority of anxiety, accusation, and condemnation.

What It Means to Declare and Decree

For many years, when I heard believers use the words "declare and decree," it seemed rather formal. Why not just say, "I pray" or "Hey, Lord, here's what I want"?

I discovered that to "declare" is to make known what you already have. At customs checkpoints at international airports, travelers declare the items in their luggage. For example, when you enter the U.S., you need to declare items you have purchased, inherited, or bought in duty-free shops, as well as products you intend to use or sell in your business.

In the same way, when we pray, we can declare what already belongs to us. "I'm a friend of God. The Holy Spirit is within me. I'm greatly loved." We declare our identity in Christ—"I'm forgiven. I'm walking free of offense. The Holy Spirit is teaching me all truth."

When we struggle, we can make declarations that reverse our circumstances. For example, when sick or exhausted, I used to think, "God, I don't feel good today. Would You heal me?" But now, instead, I say aloud, "I declare that I'm walking in health. I'm strong. I declare that I'm on the upswing."

A "decree" is an official order given by someone with governmental power. When you make a decree, you speak out what's happening "on earth as it is in heaven." You activate in the natural what has already been accomplished in the supernatural.

When I get hurt in conflicts with my family, I decree that God is leading, and I'm in sync with Him. I decree His unconditional love and joy at the center of our relationships, and His unconditional love flows even when I don't feel it in my emotions. When a thought creeps into my head that says, "I don't feel super happy right now!" I decree this anyway: "I love my kids. We're growing to be more like Christ. God's presence is changing us." Then I practice His presence and expect positive changes, collapsing a few quiffs along the way!

When my finances took downward turns, I used to pray,

"God, would You please bring more work to our software business? Help our finances. We have bills to pay." But now Tim and I declare and decree blessings, massive favor, and expansion for our customers and their clients. "The Lord is filling storehouses from the heavens, and blessing the work of our hands!"

It took a lot of practice, but slowly, gradually, I began to believe the declarations. Why? Because they weren't Lynn-truths. They were *God*-truths.

Seven Ways to Shift the Atmosphere

Why not just *think* God-truths? Why do we need to *voice* them? Because speaking them aloud demonstrates that we agree with what *He's* accomplishing. Coming into alignment with what God is saying will make a tremendous impact.

Declare and decree His promises and precipitate seven important shifts.

Fill the atmosphere with powerful sound waves. Did you know that one of the names of the devil is "prince of the power of the air"? He's out to stomp the air waves with darkness. His objective is to kidnap our atmosphere with negativity. We've got to proactively take it back. *"So then faith comes by hearing, and hearing by the word of God"* (Romans 10:17 NKJV). Sound waves can be filled with love and trust or with negative emotions, like fear or anger. Charging the atmosphere aloud with assuring words activates a faith-shift that you can use to your advantage to create an environment that fosters self-directed grace.

Shine your light. *"You will also decree a thing, and it will be established for you; and light will shine on your ways"* (Job 22:28 NASB). God-truths we decree are established with authority, because they come from our position as royals living in the Kingdom. The result is light shining on our ways because they're His ways.

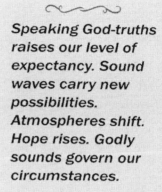

Speaking God-truths raises our level of expectancy. Sound waves carry new possibilities. Atmospheres shift. Hope rises. Godly sounds govern our circumstances.

"The LORD wraps himself in light" (Psalm 104:2). When we decree a truth, we are one with Christ, wrapping ourselves in His light. One with Him, we can see with greater discernment and the wisdom that comes from heaven, which carries the unconditional love we need to forgive ourselves.

I set out each day to be an intentional atmosphere changer. When I go into a store, I make a point of complimenting the clerks. I take time to notice what they're doing right. If they're fast, I thank them for their speed. If they point out where to find an unusual item in the store, I remark on their memory. In grocery stores, I sometimes request lunch meat at the deli. When the clerk weighs the meat, I grin and tell her that if estimating weight was an Olympic event, she'd take the gold medal. I hum *The Star-Spangled Banner* and tell her it's playing just for her!

At that moment, joy is introduced into her day. And that joy often bounces right back to me with a smile or a joke, regardless of how the day began. And you know what? My thoughts tumble one over another with the affirmation of self-acceptance in an atmosphere like that.

Cancel the great deceiver's lies. With our words, we can declare, "I cancel the assignment of the deceiver against me. I'm in a safe place with Jesus. I cancel any attack to divert me from His purposes for me in this. I void every message from the darkness in my mind and replace it with the presence and power of the Almighty One and His Word. I come to worship the Lord Most High. And in worship, only truth can reach me!"

Putting on the armor of God will equip us to stand against the schemes of the prince of the power of the air. *"For our struggle is not against flesh and blood, but against the rulers, against the authorities, against the powers of this dark world and against the spiritual forces of evil in the heavenly realms"* (Ephesians 6:12).

When we declare that our struggle is not against flesh and blood—not even against ourselves—but against the spiritual source of evil, we shift false blame from ourselves to where it belongs. The enemy is subjected to Jesus, who makes him a footstool beneath His feet (see Luke 20:43).

Bring truth into existence. Our Creator *"gives life to the dead and calls into being that which does not exist"* (Romans 4:17 NASB). His promises are always fulfilled in His time. When we speak those promises as though they're already fulfilled, we return His words to Him. *"My word . . . shall not return to Me void, but it shall accomplish what I please, and it shall prosper in the thing for which I sent it"* (Isaiah 55:11 NKJV).

We come into alignment with His eternal purposes. We trust that He's been faithful to us in the past. And then we declare that He will speak to us again in His time.

Bring about change with hope-filled words. *"What is the kingdom of God like? What shall I compare it to? It is like a mustard seed, which a man took and planted in his garden. It grew and became a tree, and the birds perched in its branches"* (Luke 13:18–19). When we speak aloud to a problem—with faith only the size of a mustard seed—we exercise our authority and strengthen our souls. Speaking the truth introduces excitement in anticipation for breakthrough. Declaring God's provision moves things from possibility to actuality. Do you want to see miracles unfold before you? Prime your mind and speak out words that change your world!

Reroute events in the natural. *"If you say to this mountain, 'Be removed and be cast into the sea,' it will be done. And whatever things you ask in prayer, believing, you will receive"* (Matthew 21:21–22 NKJV). The unmovable and unchangeable pick up and move when we speak to them. Declarations move mountains. What we say brings the possibility of tomorrow into the actuality of today. When we speak what hasn't happened as though it already has, we create a shift. Remember, *"Death and life are in the power of the tongue"* (Proverbs 18:21 KJV). What are we giving life to?

Expectant faith releases life. Jesus told His disciples, *"The words that I speak to you are spirit, and they are life"* (John 6:63 NKJV). The Bible brings us fresh life, because it is the voice of hope. When we declare and decree with expectancy and our hearts are filled with gratitude for the fulfillment of God's promises, our relationship will deepen with the Fulfiller Himself.

I've had articles published in numerous periodicals.

After a piece is written and polished, as I prepare to submit it to the editor, I ask the Lord to quiet my thoughts. I pray aloud for the souls the article will reach, even if that means only the editorial staff.

"Lord, thank You for what You're releasing as Your Word and Your Spirit go forward through these words. This is the confidence I have: that if I ask anything according to Your will, You hear me. I'm asking that readers will have a more meaningful relationship with You and learn more about Your nature."

The articles I write aren't perfect, but His Spirit is. We are stewards of those words. Spoken words pulse with the energy of His presence.

Core Truth: Speaking God-truths out loud changes the atmosphere and attracts positive changes in our circumstances.

Let's Pray

Lord, I declare and decree that I'm shifting the atmosphere with my words—in sync with Your voice. I speak to the mountains trying to hinder me and clear them from my path with a word. I press forward, decreeing that I'm forgiven! I declare a fresh love for myself and others. When things become tough and seemingly impossible, I declare that with You all things are possible.

Take the Next Step

Write a list of three battles you're engaged in. Write a declaration for each and say aloud, "With You, God, all things are possible. I declare _____ (His truth for this moment). God of limitless resources, thank You for releasing Your power here and now."

Section Three

Authority:
Take the Upper Hand

Lessons in Authority from Snakes, Bees, and Monkeys

I have given you authority to tread on serpents and scorpions, and over all the power of the enemy, and nothing shall hurt you.

Luke 10:19 (ESV)

One sunny November afternoon, Tim and I took a brisk walk on a road that flanks the Willamette River, one of our favorite places to hang out. I lifted my foot, drew in a sharp breath, and recoiled.

"Look! There's a snake in the road!"

"Where?"

I pointed to a snake the same color as the street. The poor fellow didn't have his wits about him. He'd made the fatal mistake of gliding into the path of a car.

Lessons from a Dead Snake

Here's what I learned about authority from that snake.

Fear has no authority. Fear thinks it outpowers us. But in a showdown between a 5,000-pound sedan and a five-ounce slitherer, guess who wins? When we speak out Scripture, we crush fear because *we're* the heavyweights. Here's a good verse to declare and decree: *"In Him, I have been made complete, and He is the head over all rule and authority"* (Colossians 2:10 NASB). Does Jesus tell us to jump out of the way when we see a snake coming? No. He tells us to crush it.

The great deceiver is a camouflage artist. Evil tries to blend in undetected with its surroundings. Since the snake's color nearly matched that of the asphalt, I almost stepped on it. The enemy is like that. He likes to mix truth with untruth so that, in the process, what goes unseen is never exposed, and we carry on with business as usual.

We can seize authority. The sting of danger hovers near death, but it can't touch us when we exercise authority over it. When I bent over to look at the snake, bees swarmed the little carcass. I drew back, because I'm allergic to bee stings. Was I scared of the bees? No. I said out loud, "Bees, you will not sting me. You will not touch me. I command you—go! In the name of Jesus!" I took authority over the bees. They got the message and buzzed off.

What the Bible Says About Authority

When you approach an intersection, a green light normally invites you to drive through. But what if there's been an accident and a police officer is standing there, holding out his hand, signaling you to stop? You have to halt. His authority supersedes the traffic light.

When we need help, we don't have to ask. We don't need to beg. We can proceed with certainty, because the power of all heaven backs us up when we speak Jesus' name. Jesus said, *"All authority in heaven and on earth has been given to me"* (Matthew 28:18 ESV). Because Christ lives inside us, all that belongs to Him—all authority in heaven and earth—belongs to us.

So when we say, "Stop!" every being has to halt.

"And these signs will accompany those who believe: in my name they will cast out demons; they will speak in new tongues" (Mark 16:17 ESV). When we wrestle with insecurity,

> **Authority exercised with humility, and obedience accepted with delight are the very lines along which our spirits live.**[1]
> **~ C.S. Lewis**

we can say to ourselves, "I might be having a hard day, but Jesus in me isn't! I confess that when I've been hard on myself, I've been partnering with the devil, and I repent. I believe and receive Your forgiveness, Lord!

"By the authority of the name of Jesus Christ, self-resentment, self-accusation, self-condemnation, self-criticism, self-judgment, self-contempt, self-rejection, self-blame, self-pity, and self-bitterness: get lost! Go where Jesus sends you."

"As for you, you were dead in your transgressions and sins, in which you used to live when you followed the ways of this world and of the ruler of the kingdom of the air, the spirit who is now at work in those who are disobedient" (Ephesians 2:1–2).

We need to be obedient when we hear the Lord's commands. Open disobedience invites trouble. But when we walk in accordance with His directives, no matter how much or how little sense they make, we defeat the devil. Operating out of our true authority in Christ, we smash the enemy. He stands no chance against the power of God Almighty expressed in us.

Releasing Angels

We have the authority to release angels in the heavenlies. One of the Lord's nicknames is Jehovah Sabaoth, Commander-in-Chief of the armies of heaven. He speaks with authority and gives assignments to the angels. On the earth, we can come into agreement with God's plans and step forward with confidence in our assignments.

Warrior angels help us do battle and take ground for the Kingdom. Many times when I feel insecure, I declare and decree that angels are stepping onto the scene. I gain the confidence to forge forward with angelic troops beside me.

Give It Back, in the Name of Jesus

One of my favorite children's stories is a folktale called *Caps for Sale.*[2] I must have read the story to Ben, Andy, and Emily hundreds of times. In the story, a cap salesman walks through town with checkered, gray, brown, blue, and red caps stacked on top of his head.

He calls, "Caps! Caps for Sale! Fifty cents a cap!" But no one wants to buy caps that day, so he takes a nap beneath a tree. When he wakes up, all he has is his own cap. To his dismay, in the tree branches overhead, he finds monkeys who have stolen his other caps.

"You monkeys, you," he says, shaking a finger at them, "You give me back my caps."

The monkeys shake their fingers back at him and say, "Tsz, Tsz, tsz."

Angry, the peddler repeats his request. "You monkeys, you," he says, shaking both hands, "You give me back my caps."

The monkeys mimic him and shake both their hands back at him. "Tsz, Tsz, tsz."

The peddler is furious, so he stamps his feet and repeats his demand. Then, of course, the monkeys stamp their feet right back.

Andy, who was four, had heard the story so many times that he knew what came next. To my surprise, one night he pointed to the monkeys in the picture book and exclaimed, "You monkeys, you! Give me back my caps, *in the name of Jesus!*"

I tilted my head back and roared with laughter. Andy got it. He knew how to bring everyone and everything—even miscreant monkeys—into alignment with Kingdom authority. (The story ends with the peddler throwing his cap to the ground in frustration. The monkeys do the same with their caps. They come toppling down from the tree, and the peddler scoops them up. The caps, that is—not the monkeys.)

All of creation must give back what was stolen, in the name of Jesus!

Take Charge of Your Thoughts and Words!

Take authority over the thoughts and words the devil puts in your head as he tries to steal, kill, and destroy. Because you have new life in Christ, His abundant life lives inside you. His thoughts and words are yours. Declare them!

> *Far above all rule and authority and power and dominion . . .*
> *He put all things in subjection under His feet.*
> Ephesians 1:21–22 NASB

The enemy's under your foot. Go ahead. Crush him. Forgive yourself.

Core Truth: When we exercise our authority in Christ, we readily defeat the schemes of the enemy.

Let's Pray

Lord, I walk in Your authority and power. I submit my circumstances to Your will. I sit at Your right hand and join You in crushing the enemies, making them a footstool under my feet (Psalm 110:1). *"The kingdom of heaven suffers violence, and violent men take it by force* (Matthew 11:12 NASB).

By the authority of the name of Jesus Christ, I take charge of my thoughts and words. They belong to You! I'm forgiven and I forgive myself. I thank You and praise You, Father, for the authority You have given me to release angels. *"For You will command Your angels concerning me* to guard me in all my ways; they will lift me up in their hands, so that I will not strike my foot against a stone" (Psalm 91:11–12).

Take the Next Step

On a cardboard tube or rolled page, write an accusation that has come against you. On a separate page, write the declaration: "Jesus has given _____ (your name) authority to tread on serpents and scorpions, and over all the power of the enemy. By the power of His name, _____ (accusation) has lost its power. God has prevailed!"

Put the tube on the floor and crush it with your foot. Read your declaration aloud. What shift is taking place?

---

[1]C.S. Lewis. *The Weight of Glory.* Harper Collins. 2009. p. 115.

[2]Esphyr Slobodkina. *Caps for Sale.* Harper Collins. 1987

The Enemy Will Show You Where to Fight

The thief comes only to steal and kill and destroy. I came that they may have life and have it abundantly.

John 10:10 (ESV)

Friend, do you want to know one of the best ways to frustrate the devil as you work through self-forgiveness? Pay close attention to what he's saying! It will give you the upper hand.

Discover What Makes Jesus Laugh

When we hear, "I can't do it. I'm not making any progress," we need to look for growth. Welcome the invitation to dial in the GPS coordinates on the battlefield where we're contending—the sweet spot where our Healer is releasing the supernatural.

In a second car accident, in 2013, I was rear-ended on a freeway off-ramp, and my car was crushed as it was pushed into the car ahead of me. In the weeks that followed, my badly injured legs, back and neck kept me from climbing stairs or taking long walks. I suffered a nasty head injury. Headaches, memory loss, confusion, and wobbly legs made it hard to return to work. I was frustrated and impatient with the healing process.

At dinner one night with my family, I fought uninvited tears. Weary of constant headaches, I dropped my chin into the palm of my hand.

I prayed without words, simply opening my mind to Christ's presence.

In my heart, I heard Him softly ask, "Are you feeling stuck?"

I replied, "Yes. I'm not making any headway."

"That thought isn't from me. It's from the devil." I thought I heard Him laugh.

I said, "Wait! What's so funny?"

Again, I heard Him laugh, only louder this time. "You are stronger today than you were yesterday. Here's a surge of energy, right from heaven."

I thought, "Is it possible? Am I stronger? That doesn't make sense.

"There have been a lot of times in the past when I didn't 'get' You, but I went along anyway. Okay. Let me try something I couldn't do before."

Rising from the dinner table, I hobbled down the stairs to my basement, where I worked out on my recumbent bike and stretched my muscles, declaring that I was making a comeback. Remarkably, my headache lifted. I found more flexibility in my back. My legs had a greater range of motion. I felt the strength in my neck and arm muscles returning. Then I climbed the stairs on my own.

When I returned to the chiropractor the next day, he said I was on my way to a rapid recovery. I broke into a broad grin. Where was that battle won? In my mind. Who showed me where to fight? The prince of darkness.

Find out how evil opens the dialogue. Then, take up the topic with Christ. Enter into the spirit of His joy and expect to take back aggressive ground.

Convert a Dark Room into a Darkroom

Before the age of the digital camera, photographs were produced from film developed in a darkroom. Black turned white. Red turned green. Blue turned orange. When the deceiver shows us an image of our identity and holds it up with a smug, "Ta-da!" as though it were finished, we need to come into deliberate agreement with the lie's precise opposite.

As I recovered, I struggled with loneliness and isolation. I flipped through cards that friends and family had sent. I felt the Holy Spirit say, "Let's spend the next few nights writing out words of encouragement."

I laughed. "You want *me* to encourage *them*?"

"That's right."

"Okay. You call the shots. My handwriting might be shaky. With my headaches, I might not spell everything right. But why not? Let's do it."

When I heard the father of lies say that I was lonely and isolated, I realized I had a choice. I could believe him or purpose to live with companionship and connectedness. I committed to putting my energy into my relationships.

I wrote encouraging notes to two friends a day. Later, they told me that the cards uplifted and cheered them. They said that they felt close to me. And when they expressed their friendship with hugs and smiles, I felt connected with them. My encouragement drew the cords of our relationships closer together.

> **When we forgive, we bring in light where there was darkness. We summon positives to replace negatives. We open the door to an unseen future that our painful past had shut.[1]**
> ~ Lewis Smedes

When you're in an emotional place that feels like a "dark room," realize that God has granted you access into the "darkroom" so that you can get a better picture of the enemy's position, strategize in that very area, and come into alignment with its precise opposite.

Find the Coordinates for Your Battle

When you look in the mirror and are tempted to call yourself a failure, look instead at how God is shaping you. Every time a negative thought such as resentment, shame, or condemnation enters your mind, turn it around. Declare the God-given truth for your future.

God-truth originates from His Word. It declares that you're patient with yourself. It hopes and believes for growth. God-truth expects a great outcome!

When the devil chatters in your head, nod and lean forward, pencil hovering over your journal. Ask, "Where on

the battlefield do I need to position myself next?"
Watch him scowl and back away.
Disciple: One. Devil: Zero.

Core Truth: The enemy will show us where we are about to make gains.

Let's Pray

Holy Spirit, as I enter the battle, which part of my identity is in the accuser's crosshairs? What's the lie? I'm grateful for HD clarity of its exact opposite. I resolve to rehearse God-truths from the Bible to show me promises of who I'm becoming. I accept Your vote of confidence. No matter what the devil says, I'm forgiven. I forgive myself. Thank you for God-truths of gentleness and mercy. I purpose to take self-directed kindness to the next level.

Take the Next Step

Draw a colored map of the battlefield where you are warring against the forces of darkness. Add hills and rivers. Where have you been injured the most? Ask the Holy Spirit what He's eliminating in battle. Label the hills and rivers with key words. Ask Him why your attention is being drawn to those sectors. What is He depositing?

---

[1]Lewis Smedes. *The Art of* Forgiving. Ballantine Books. 1997. p.176.

Are You Prosecutor, Defendant, and Judge?

It is the Lord who judges me. Therefore judge nothing before the appointed time; wait until the Lord comes. He will bring to light what is hidden in darkness and will expose the motives of the heart. At that time each will receive their praise from God.

1 Corinthians 4:4–5

Before a packed courtroom, prosecuting attorney Jan stands in a crisp navy dress suit. With a fistful of files, she strides to the front of the room, announcing that the arraignment has begun. She reads the charges. The room fills with tension.

Then, without warning, Jan crosses the aisle and drops into a seat at the defense table. Her shoulders slump. She listens to the charges. Color rises in her cheeks. Her head drops to her chest.

But then a minute later, Jan rushes behind the bench, pulls on a robe and glasses, and takes a seat. She scowls and silences murmurs with three taps of her gavel.

"Order in the court. Defendant, today you're charged with a serious crime. How do you plead?"

Jan doesn't wait for an answer. She quickly throws off the robe and glasses, drops them onto the bench, and dashes back to her chair at the defense table.

She covers her face with her hands. In a barely audible voice, she whispers, "Guilty."

Absurd? Maybe. Who'd run around a courtroom and play the role of prosecutor, defendant, and judge all at once? How ridiculous!

But that's exactly what we do when we accuse ourselves.

Whose Side Are You on, Anyway?

When we appoint ourselves prosecutor, we high-five the devil. We enter into agreement with his accusation and condemnation. That weakens us on every level. "Look what my actions cost," we say to ourselves. "I injured other people, and I hurt myself. I deserve what I've got coming."

When we accept accusation from the father of lies, in effect, we shrug off the promise that we've been set free. *"Therefore, there is now no condemnation for those who are in Christ Jesus, because through Christ Jesus the law of the Spirit who gives life has set me free from the law of sin and death"* (Romans 8:1–2).

Condemnation and the grace of Christ can't co-exist in the same space. Christ shed His blood for us, and His sacrifice is complete. So we can hold our heads high, knowing we are greatly loved and greatly forgiven. Let's appropriate what He paid for!

Only one judge can occupy the bench at a time. When we take on the role of judge, we demand that the Lord empty His seat so that we can take His place. Punishing ourselves for mistakes says, "God's not the judge. I am. My authority is greater than His."

> To forgive yourself is to act out the mystery of one person who is both forgiver and forgiven.[1]
> ~ Lewis Smedes

Layer upon Layer of Pain

I was guilty of accusing myself, but I worked hard to hide it. When I related to people, I kept up my guard. The outside layer of my emotions was a wall of shame. I put up a barrier so others couldn't see my struggle. The layer beneath was anger and control. Because I'd been hurt as a kid, I tried to protect myself from further pain. When I was hurt anyway, I turned the anger inward and pushed it down—hard.

The next layer was fear. I was afraid I'd lose my friends if they knew what I was really like. When business was slow, I was fearful we'd lose our house. When I ran late for appointments, I succumbed to anxiety attacks. The core emotion in my heart was self-directed resentment. I felt powerless to let go of my failures.

Those layers of shame, anger, fear, and self-directed resentment were drawn to the surface over and over. I was painfully aware of those emotions and hated to see them exposed.

Put Down the Superhero Cape and Back Away Slowly

When I got in trouble, I tried to cover it up. At a business training, when the content got technical and confusing, I nodded as though I understood every word. At church, when we worshiped, I sometimes sang the wrong lyrics. At a prayer conference, I interrupted a meeting with uncontrollable laughter. When I drew funny stares, I worked to divert attention away from myself as quickly as I could.

Afterwards, I slid behind the steering wheel of my car and pressed my palms to my cheeks.

I thought, "Wow, way to go."

I heard a voice in my head. "Who do you think you are, Mrs. Superhero?"

"Uh, no." I bit my lip. "I don't have superpowers. I just crave people's approval." I frowned. I hadn't been entirely honest about my mistakes with others. I'd put on my game face and hoped no one noticed.

I figured I was probably being judged, so I judged myself, hoping to beat others to the punch.

But the Word is clear: *"There is only one Lawgiver and Judge, the one who is able to save and destroy. But you— who are you to judge your neighbor?"* (James 4:12). Who are we to judge our neighbors? Who are we to judge *ourselves*? He alone is Judge of all the earth. In His legal courtroom, He weighs the evidence and reaches a decision. We agree to accept His verdict.

> **It's time to extend the compassion that you have felt for others to yourself.**[2]
> ~ Dr. Robert Enright

The Evidence Is In

When we are tempted to accuse ourselves, we need to examine what the Word of God says.

The blood of Christ covers us. *"How much more will the blood of Christ, who through the eternal Spirit offered himself without blemish to God, purify our conscience from dead works to serve the living God"* (Hebrews 9:14 ESV).

The penalty has already been paid on the cross. *"He is the propitiation for our sins"* (1 John 2:2 ESV). Father God sacrificed His Son so that we no longer have to pay for our iniquities.

When we repent, forgiveness is ours. *"For whenever our heart condemns us, God is greater than our heart, and he knows everything"* (1 John 3:20 ESV). God sees our sin. He knows all about it. Following our repentance, He wipes the slate clean.

We have two Advocates in the courtroom. The first is the Holy Spirit:

"He who searches our hearts knows the mind of the Spirit, because the Spirit intercedes for God's people in accordance with the will of God" (Romans 8:27). The other is Christ Himself: *"Christ Jesus who died—more than that, who was raised to life—is at the right hand of God and is also interceding for us"* (Romans 8:34).

On the days when the accuser is relentless, we can declare his destination: *"For the accuser of our brothers and sisters has been thrown down to earth—the one who accuses them before our God day and night"* (Revelation 12:10 NLT).

Christ overcame our adversary. Regardless of where our

emotions go, it's our job to agree with what He has already accomplished.

The Charges Are Dropped

Our Righteous Judge takes His place at the bench. *Tap! Tap! Tap!* The sound of His gavel arrests the attention of everyone in the crowded courtroom. The Judge declares that His Son's sacrifice has covered the charges and paid your penalty. You owe nothing. You're free to go. Court adjourned.

You lift your head and leap to your feet. You give Jesus a broad grin and pump His hand. Pressing past the cameras, microphones, and the clamoring press, you thrust open the double doors and jog down the steps to the sidewalk. Raising your arms to heaven, you take a deep breath, tilt your head back, and laugh.

You're free!

Core Truth: The courtroom bench belongs only to God the Judge.

Let's Pray

Father, I'm sorry for partnering with the accuser and condemning myself. I give up the right to judge myself. I release any sense of guilt and shame, and I break from self-judgment. Your resurrection power lives in me.

"If our hearts do not condemn us, we have confidence before You and receive from You anything we ask" (1 John 3:21–22). Father, fill me and my home with Your justice. I

accept Your wide, long, high, and deep love and forgiveness. I'm free!

Take the Next Step

Draw a picture of Attorney Jesus in a courtroom, standing before God the Judge at the bench on your behalf. Sketch the Holy Spirit at your side. At the top of the picture, write a short word or phrase that tells the charge against you, the truth Jesus is bringing to your defense, and the word "free!"

At the foot of the page write, *"Therefore there is now no condemnation for those who are in Christ Jesus"* (Romans 8:1).

---

[1]Lewis B. Smedes. Forgive & Forget: Healing the Hurts We Don't Deserve. HarperCollins. 1996. p. 77.

[2]Dr. Robert Enright. 8 Keys to Forgiveness. W. W. Norton and Company. 2015. p. 188.

The Power of a Key Scripture

*Keep this Book of the Law always on your
lips; meditate on it day and night, so that
you may be careful to do everything written
in it. Then you will be prosperous and
successful.*

Joshua 1:8

Sometimes, when we're mid-battle in our minds, victory comes in the form of a strategic Bible verse. The Lord invites us to edify, exhort, and comfort one another (see 1 Corinthians 14:3). "Edifying" means "building up." When we spend time reading God's Word, He reinforces our understanding of His power and our faith is fortified.

Exhorting is all about encouraging. When He commands us to forgive ourselves, He exhorts our hearts to rise up and out of discouragement to a place of Holy Spirit expansion. The Holy Spirit comforts our hearts with His counsel as He quietly touches the raw pain deep within us and heals our inner wounds.

Writing a Crafted Prayer

An outstanding book about interacting with key Scriptures is Graham Cooke's *Crafted Prayer: The Joy of Always Getting Your Prayers Answered*. Graham underlines the importance of praying the will of God, which brings us into a place of faith and proclamation. We take key verses and write—or "craft"—them into a prayer.

Graham says, "Crafted prayer is a wonderful tool. We can look at our situation, take time to study the Word, take time for thanksgiving, and bring our heart into line with what God wants to do. Then we craft a prayer that covers the whole issue."[1] He invites us to write out the prayer and share it with others. Then, Graham says, the prayer will release God's greatness, majesty and inheritance in us.

A Prayer that Paints a Picture

I often talk to the Lord about my parenting. For years, I used to raise my voice at my son Andy when he didn't meet my expectations. But instead of making things better, yelling made them worse. He withdrew.

Later, he told me that I'd made such a big deal about my dislike for the movies he and his friends had watched at our house, he felt like they were unwelcome. He gave one-word answers when I tried to connect with him. He froze up when I tried to give him a hug.

Night after night, I tossed and turned, but my runaway thoughts weren't about him—they were about me. They accused and condemned me. As I reviewed each day in my mind's eye, I saw my crossed arms, a scowl between my eyebrows, and tension in my neck. Anger flashed across the room. No wonder he didn't want to talk to me!

For almost a year, I asked my divine Counselor how to mend my relationship with Andy.

He directed me to Hebrews 10: 35–36: *"So do not throw away your confidence; it will be richly rewarded. You need to persevere so that when you have done the will of God, you will receive what he has promised."*

Based on the verses, I wrote a crafted prayer:

God, thank You, thank You, thank You!
As I listen in on Your grace-filled godhead table chat,
That hope-filled dialogue transforms me.
The fruit of Your promises brings my heart to trust.
Renew my steadfast confidence in You.
As I learn Your plan, I persevere and seek Your rich rewards.
On the canvas atop its easel, may Your hand of kindness
Paint me a picture of self-forgiving mercy
And the joy-filled heart of an Unshakable Warrior.

I gained the most ground when I meditated on those verses. I closed my eyes and focused on them while I was in line at the store, on hold for a business call, and as I was getting the mail out of my mailbox. I read them aloud to Jesus just before I began conversations with my kids.

Fresh surges of perseverance in seeking God's rewards in the relationship rose up in my soul.

One morning, in my quiet time, I asked Jesus to paint

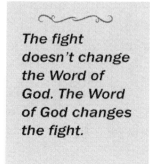

The fight doesn't change the Word of God. The Word of God changes the fight.

me a picture of self-forgiving mercy. In my mind's eye, I saw the picture of a warrior, down on one knee, sword and shield before her, head bowed. The warrior in the painting was humble but filled with honor. I had the sense that the Redeemer forgave me. I knew then that I could forgive myself.

Warring with Humility

On the white board over my dining room table, I wrote: *"For the Lord delights in his people; he crowns the humble with victory"* (Psalm 149:4 NLT). I meditated on the verse every time I ate. He whispered in my heart, "Humility is the key. It will turn everything around."

Instead of shrinking back with mistrust and apprehension, I relaxed and approached Andy with a fresh kindness and love. I spoke with him gently and apologized for my anger. In my mind, I pictured the joy-filled heart of an unshakable warrior.

And guess what? He sensed it and responded with newfound warmth. He forgave me. Mutual acceptance was a reward in and of itself.

And once we were back "on" again, when my head hit the pillow at night, Jesus seemed to be smiling. I drifted off to sleep, liking myself a little better.

The Word of God Is a Forever Thing

I used to think that spending time reading and listening to Bible verses was just a matter of discipline so that Father

God would know I was familiarizing myself with His "Best of" series. I figured the 66 books contained within the Bible were a top-shelf read. But now I know differently. Scripture is a marvelous, pulsing energy that lives, breathes, and electrifies.

The more time you and I spend with our relentless, unshakable Savior, the more we sense Him in His Word. We recognize a steady presence—stable and unmovable. Regardless of the reaction of those around us, when we anchor ourselves with Bible verses, a significant shift happens.

In *Crafted Prayer*, Graham Cooke invites us to "Meditate on God, waiting for Him to speak. He will give you key words and phrases and a sense of His objective. Then He might supplement that with Scripture or pictures. Write everything down, as it comes to you. As you do, a peace will fall on you, and a confidence will begin to rise in your spirit."[2]

Getting it Straight with a Spirit Level

When Tim and I hang a new picture in our home, we use a measuring instrument called a "spirit level" to make sure it's hung straight. A spirit level is a tool used to indicate how parallel (level) or perpendicular (plumb) a surface is relative to the earth. The name of the tool comes from the mineral spirit solution inside the curved tube. The liquid is set so that the air bubble rests between two marks on the tube when the tool is perfectly horizontal.

A similar instrument is introduced into the supernatural equation when we pray the Word of God. Prayer teams I serve on often release unity, restoration, forgiveness, and healing for individuals and groups of people. At casual coffee shop meetings, missions conferences, business seminars, worship gatherings, and Saturday morning prayer walks, our teams love to see the city come to life—by praying the Word of God.

When we speak out Scripture, we come into alignment with the wisdom of all heaven. I can't count the number of times I've prayed into the wisdom that's pure, peace-loving, considerate, submissive, full of mercy and good fruit, impartial and sincere (James 3:17).

We gain power when we agree with Scripture that every good and perfect gift is from above, coming down from our Father of heavenly lights (see James 1:17). We release joy and laughter, even when things go south. Especially when they do! When we bring the Word of God into our prayers, that "spirit level" is at work. We find that sweet spot where we are on an even keel.

Often, when I quote Scripture, I can sense a shift in a person. The furrow in her forehead smoothes. A smile tugs at the corners of her mouth. The Word of God serves as the "spirit level." Things are put right, though not always predictably!

Do we need to be perfect? No. But we know Him who is Perfect Love. When we focus on a Bible verse, pray it, and allow it to come to life in our relationships, we gain victory. The result is an atmosphere that fosters massive grace.

Core Truth: Praying key Scriptures releases strength for our next steps.

Let's Pray

Thank You, Father, for Your Word. Direct me to a passage and use it to transform me. Paint me a picture of who I'm becoming with that verse. Your Word is a forever thing! Scripture speaks to me, and through it, I receive Your love and return it with all my heart, soul, mind, and strength. Your Word lives and breathes in me. My confidence level rises as I persevere in forgiving myself. Holy Spirit, illuminate the next step for me—found in Your Word. Bring it to life!

Take the Next Step

Ask the Holy Spirit for a personal Scripture for you in this season. Write it out. Then write a short, crafted prayer of about seven lines based on the passage. Pray it through as the Holy Spirit leads. Keep your key Scripture and crafted prayer on an app and access them regularly. Actively work to commit them to memory. Meditate on them.

---

[1]Graham Cooke. *Crafted Prayer: The Joy of Always Getting Your Prayers Answered.* 2003. p. 37.

[2]Ibid., p. 61.

Section Four

Healing:
Find Your Safe Place

To Forgive Yourself,
Forgive Others

*For he has . . . brought us into the kingdom
of the Son he loves, in whom we have
redemption, the forgiveness of sins.*
                                    Colossians 1:13–14

Following my car accident with Ben, waves of exhaustion rolled over me. I needed physical therapy to regain muscle strength and endurance. But even more, I needed emotional balance. In God's gym, I needed to build up my forgiveness muscles.

I'd been on my back for days. When the day arrived for me to begin to get back on my feet, I sat up on my hospital bed and took slow, painstaking turns. As I swung my legs around to sit up, my ribs howled. My neck and back throbbed with pain.

A stern-faced nurse gave me the task of taking my first steps. As my feet touched the cold tiled floor, I wobbled and teetered. I mumbled something about the accident. She raised her voice and demanded to know what sin I'd committed to deserve such judgment from God. My face burned and my stomach lurched. Her words knocked the wind out of me. I couldn't tell if my legs trembled because I was so weak or because her remark shook me up. Maybe both.

At a friend's potluck a few weeks later, several couples discussed my gradual recovery. I told them that I'd taken my eyes off the road to pull a rattle out of Ben's hand. I described his head injury and the seizures that followed. A woman turned to me and loudly announced, "Well, I hope you learned your lesson!"

I felt humiliated. The sting of the self-condemning thoughts I'd been dealing with were painful enough, but her words were like daggers that penetrated my soul, hard and deep. "All those things I've accused myself of must be true," I thought. "God's judging me. He's angry. No wonder I can't sleep at night."

The tension in my emotions spilled over into my relationship with the Savior, and I realized that I needed to forgive the women who'd condemned me—not for their sakes, but for mine. I didn't realize it at the time, but if I could let go of the resentment embedded in my thoughts, I'd be in a better position to release myself from my own self-directed bitterness.

It took years for me to reach a place where I could forgive them. My self-talk reinforced a humiliation I'd experienced and taken on as my own.

How Forgiving Others Helps Us Forgive Ourselves

True forgiveness isn't about a contrived, forced erasure of offenses. It doesn't mean that we pretend an event didn't happen. Our memories carry emotions, both positive and negative. But in order to think and pray clearly, we need to let go of hurts inflicted by others.

Forgiving ourselves is more easily done by those who have first forgiven others.[1]

~R.T. Kendall

Forgiving others is one of the best moves we can make, because it helps us forgive ourselves. Here's how.

When we forgive, our relationship with the Lord flows without interruption. Unfinished business opens the door for resentment to build in our hearts. When we pray, that bitterness blocks the flow of dialogue. *"Make allowance for each other's faults, and forgive anyone who offends you. Remember, the Lord forgave you, so you must forgive others"* (Colossians 3:13 NLT).

When we forgive others' offenses, we clear distractions and hindrances from our dialogues with Jesus. Praying from a position of grace, our minds, wills, and emotions operate more clearly and with more wisdom as we chat with Jesus about our plans.

Each act of reconciliation matures us. When we're in conflict with people, it's natural to want to withdraw. Often—but not always—Christ directs us to reconcile. We can gently go to others and talk things out.

I take each hurt to Christ. He drops hints about people's weaknesses. He points out that the more hurtful they are, the more likely it is that they feel insecure, inadequate, and wounded. Hurt people hurt people. When we ask Him to show us how to resolve a conflict, He will direct us to the path of peace. That peace will naturally spill over into moments when we're alone.

Reconciliation clears the atmosphere. A rift in a relationship produces emotional tension, like cigarette smoke clouding a room. When we speak angrily with others, we add to the problem. But words of grace and kindness clear the air—which is just what we need when it comes to breathing easy with our own issues.

The enemy can't keep us up at night with unresolved anger. Do you toss and turn when you're upset? I do. When we forgive, it clears our heads, and we can sleep with Christ's peace, because we're in alignment with Him. *"Be angry and do not sin; do not let the sun go down on your anger"* (Ephesians 4:26 ESV). When we forgive those who've hurt us, we're more likely to wake up rested and refreshed with a more lighthearted view to govern how we think and speak to ourselves.

Forgiving others produces friendships we need as we learn to accept ourselves. No one can grow alone. We all need a team to keep us on course. When we forgive our friends, we're more likely to stick with them for the long haul. When we feel like giving up, friends can speak into us the love we need to accept ourselves.

Mega-Chances to Forgive Stolen Goods

I secretly wish I could skate right through conflicts like an Olympic champion gracefully doing double axels. But the truth is, I've had many hurts and offenses that landed me on my backside on the ice.

I live in a sector of Portland, Oregon where crime is on the rise. My car was stolen twice from in front of my house and once from a store parking lot. While I was helping set up a downtown prayer event in Portland, my wallet was stolen. I couldn't deny it: the path of evil had intersected with my safe world.

I realized that I had a choice to make: I could grow angry about the thefts or switch up my mindset.

I thought, "I'm so frustrated that my car is gone!" I sat with that for a while.

Then I made a shift: "But I was the one stolen from—not the one stealing."

Next, I thought about the thieves. "What were they thinking? Grand theft auto is a felony."

I quieted my emotions. "Hey, my family has another car. Yeah, I'm mad, but I'm going to pray for the criminals. They had no idea what they were in for when they messed with me!" I prayed for them to know Jesus as their best friend and for their hearts to be healed.

The police retrieved my car. I replaced my wallet, driver's license, and credit cards. I moved on. But maybe something much more precious was taken from you, like the life of a loved one. I have no idea how deep your pain runs. I am sorry for your loss.

Did you know that whenever something is stolen, you are in a position to receive sevenfold recompense? *"People do not despise a thief if he steals to satisfy his hunger when he is starving. Yet if he is caught, he must pay sevenfold, though it costs him all the wealth of his house"* (Proverbs 6:30–31). What kind of loot did the enemy make off with? Great news: you've got seven times that coming!

The Role of Friendship When We're Blindfolded

As a child, I enjoyed playing games, especially on birthdays. When I was eight years old, I attended a party where a friend invited guests to the garage for a game of Pin the Tail on the Donkey. When my turn came, the children blindfolded me and spun me around a few times. Then I set out to find the donkey.

But dizzy and disoriented, I veered off down the driveway. After a few paces, I sensed something was wrong. I removed the blindfold and found to my dismay that I was in the street! Frustrated and angry, I asked why no one had stopped me or turned me around.

We can't always make course corrections on our own. God uses friends to reveal our blind spots and help us return to His precepts. We need friends in our lives who recognize toxic thoughts of resentment or bitterness. It's important to give them permission to tell us when we need to forgive.

The feedback of those friends helps us grow and mature in Christ. The more real we are in opening up and being vulnerable about our shortcomings, the more authentic our relationship will be as they cheer us on. In fact, a genuine friend will always invite us into the freedom found in forgiving others.

Steps to Forgiving Others

- **Acknowledge the pain aloud.** What is the pain like? What has the offense cost you? Time? Money? Physical pain? What consequences are you dealing with? How did others' actions and words hurt people you love?

- **Identify your feelings.** Do you feel angry? Rejected? Confused? Depressed? Jealous? Helpless? Defensive? Overwhelmed? Disillusioned? Bitter?

- **Identify unrealistic expectations.** Did you look for the person to give you something they didn't have? Where can you lower the bar?

- **Acknowledge that Jesus died for the sins of all.** His death on the cross covers you and the person who hurt you.

- **Do a heart check. Make a decision to forgive.** You can decide to forgive the other person with your decisive will, even if your feelings aren't quite there yet. It's okay if it takes a while for your emotions to catch up.

- **Release the pain, hurt emotions, and losses.** Write them out or illustrate them. Give them to the Lord.

- **Bless the one who hurt you.** Wish them well.

- **Recognize that forgiveness is not the same as reconciliation.** Ask the Lord if reconciliation is possible, safe, or appropriate. Sometimes returning to the relationship is not the best, because the person or situation is still very harmful. Get counsel from mentors or friends when you need it. Ask the Holy Spirit. Follow His lead.

   When we release others, our self-talk makes a shift. "Hey, I'm growing. If I can forgive them, I can forgive myself."

   "Let perseverance finish its work so that you may be mature and complete, not lacking anything" (James 1:4). When we persevere in our relationships, we have

the power to speak wisdom into our own thought life. *"If it is possible, as far as it depends on you, live at peace with everyone"* (Romans 12:18). God, who is peace Himself, is releasing His calm certainty in our relationships. In the process, well-being is rewired into our minds, and healing is set in motion.

• **Acknowledge your growth.** In one of my favorite books, *Freedom Through Forgiveness,* Nathan Daniel says, "Once you forgive from the heart, you will be free to live without fear and regret. You will live in today, not looking back and trying to correct the mistakes of yesterday. Living for today means trusting God to protect you every day. If He allows you to get hurt, it means He has given you an opportunity to grow up and learn to forgive like Jesus forgave."[2]

Taking these steps to forgive others will empower you to accept and forgive yourself.

Core Truth: Forgiving others gives us freedom to forgive ourselves.

Let's Pray

Holy Spirit, I've been deeply hurt, and I struggle to forgive. Sometimes it hurts so much that forgiving doesn't make sense. Thank You for being with me in the pain. What grieves me grieves You. Here are my feelings: _____ (name them). I invite You into them.

Father, thank You for forgiving me. I need to forgive

_____. Give me the desire to want to forgive. When my emotions don't feel ready, I choose with my will to break from judging those who have hurt me. I forgive and release them. I pray they will grow. I actively forgive myself and am at peace with myself today. I am growing to be more like You. Because You live inside me, Your peace is mine.

Take the Next Step

Has someone hurt you? As the Holy Spirit brings someone to mind, write a letter to him or her and describe how it affected your heart. Then destroy the letter.

Take the steps in this chapter. Ask the Redeemer for His thoughts and heart for the person and for wisdom to guide your next steps. If it seems too hard to forgive, ask for support from a friend or trusted counselor. Seek reconciliation if the Holy Spirit leads. Is there anything you need to forgive yourself for? Write a letter of forgiveness and acceptance to yourself.

---

[1]R.T. Kendall. *How to Forgive Ourselves Totally*. Charisma House. 2007. p. 92.

[2]Nathan Daniel. *Freedom Through Forgiveness.* Vision Publishing. 2007. p. 79.

Sounds of a Brilliant Redeemer

If you call out for insight and cry aloud for understanding, and if you look for it as for silver and search for it as for hidden treasure, then you will understand the fear of the LORD and find the knowledge of God.

Proverbs 2:3-5

Freedom comes as you and I grow in our relationship with Christ. Healing is part of that growth. But for me, emotional and physical healing happened gradually. I dealt with fibromyalgia for years. Pain pummeled every muscle, tendon, ligament, and connective tissue.

Some days it felt like I had been hit by a Mac truck and was lying on my back on the shoulder of a freeway.

"Okay, Jesus," I asked, imagining my eyes sweeping the clouds above. "What do I need to do to get healed? Where's that freedom You keep talking about?"

"Listen in on conversations with your family," He replied. "But not with *your* heart. Listen with *Mine*."

I winced. I thought, "Do we have to go there?"

The Shift My Family Needed

I used to be super-critical of my family—the way they dressed, talked, stacked the dishwasher, folded towels, and arrived late for dinner. The list went on and on.

I asked Jesus, "What do they want in my relationship with them?"

His reply: "They want you to forgive yourself."

I shook my head in disbelief. "They want me to forgive *myself*? Don't they want me to forgive *them*? They're the ones who constantly blow it."

Jesus smiled and waited.

I said, "I don't know. I can be so obnoxious sometimes. Ugh! Maybe *they* need to forgive *me*. Yes, that's how a better relationship will happen."

Jesus said with a gentle voice, "They want you to forgive *yourself*. Your family wants you to be free from self-condemnation. When you 'get' My acceptance and make it your own, you connect with them from a stable, steady space. You're far more affirming and easier to live with."

"Where do I begin?"

"Listen for My voice. Accept My love."

So I listened. And then I listened some more.

Alone Time with Christ

Jesus whispered, "Make blank spaces on your calendar to spend time with Me. Let's just sit or walk together. In that space, I'll speak wisdom."

I opened up some pockets of time to spend alone with Him. When I did, He told me that I could expect His words and thoughts to saturate my heart and mind. He told me that I could bring those thoughts to my marriage, even when Tim and I had conflicts.

I used to believe that happy couples never had problems. I thought, "It must be nice to have no differences. But Tim and I disagree and some days argue when the needle on the stress-o-meter spikes."

Over time, I gradually understood that it was okay to become frustrated and even angry, but I needed to sort things out with the Holy Spirit. Mid-conflict, Tim and I still sometimes aren't on the same page. We don't seem to be in the same book. Or even the same library! When that happens, we take a break and process our thoughts separately. We make room for God to speak.

When we come back together, remarkably, there's a spirit of unity. Though we still might not agree on an issue, we affirm that we're a safe place for one another. Patient Tim has listened to my insecurities and stories late into the night. His kindness and loving responses have been the safe haven that I needed to foster a sense of self-acceptance.

Putting on the Hoodie of Praise

On days when I have a heavy heart, I empty myself and put on praise music. An unparalleled peace pervades my home. I worship when I wash the dishes, write at my computer, and have meals with my family. Some days, I take off the spirit of heaviness, which feels like a cumbersome wool coat. I exchange it for a garment of praise—a light, soft blue hoodie.

When we draw close to God, we find that there is

nothing we can do to make Him love us more or less. Jesus wants us to accept ourselves, no matter what's happened in the past. He loves our "Thank You." It opens up space in us for contentment. When we worship, His presence fills us.

Livestreaming the Holy Spirit

After 30 years of serving on prayer teams, I have bookshelves brimming with books, training manuals, CDs, DVDs, workbooks, notebooks, and journals. But I'm convinced that in spite of all those resources, in the end, our number one source of wisdom is the voice of our brilliant Redeemer.

Sometimes, when people ask for prayer, I say, "I'd be happy to sit with you at the feet of the Master and listen together."

When I pray with people, sometimes I hear a Bible verse in my mind or heart. Other times, I hear birdsong, the lapping of ocean swells on a ship's port and starboard, the *clip-clop* of horses' hooves, the *whop-whop* of helicopter propellers, or the *click* of a camera's shutter release. I don't analyze the sound. I just go with it. I share what I hear.

After I pray, people sometimes ask, "How did you do that? How did you sense those things?"

I tell them, "I turn off my television, computer, and other electronics. I clear the air waves and my mind, and then I imagine the resonant frequency of the Holy Spirit's voice. I get in sync with Him. Just as we can catch a simulcast of a live event happening on our computer screens, we can 'watch' the scene the Holy Spirit plays out in our hearts and minds and relay what we see."[1]

Sensing the Holy Spirit's Frequency

Imagine a crystal wine glass on a dining table before you. If you sing loudly at the frequency of the glass's natural resonance, your voice can make it vibrate and shatter. In the same way, we can sense the sound waves of the Holy Spirit's voice and come into alignment with them.

I like to listen to the Bible on audio as I drive. *"Faith comes by hearing, and hearing by the Word of God"* (Romans 10:17 NKJV). Later, I share what I hear.

There's a rhythm, a cadence of the Holy Spirit's flow that washes across us. The brilliant Redeemer's unique voice will bathe us with a radiant love. *"The Son is the radiance of God's glory"* (Hebrews 1:3).

> *When we enter into the thrumming vibrations of our Brilliant Redeemer's grace, we become one with His sound.*

Maybe, as Elijah found, the Redeemer's voice won't be in the wind, or earthquake, or fire, but will be in the sound of a low whisper (see 1 Kings 19:11–12). Jesus says to us, "I am Hope. Sense My presence as I wrap My arms around you." Our future is filled with our brilliant Redeemer's grace, which extends to anything we've done or will ever do.

Breath of God

With the pain of trials come quiet nights when we're left with our own thoughts. When you go to bed, do bits and bytes of mistakes from the day drift back into your mind? When the

Holy Spirit is invited into a blank moment, He leans over and breathes on us. There the sound of heaven is released.

Tonight, listen for the sound of the Holy Spirit. What does it sound like? Be prepared for something unusual. Maybe you'll hear a bicycle bell, dancing chimes, or a gurgling stream. Then again, it could be a special sound from your past that awakens you to His everywhere-at-every-time presence. Or maybe, just maybe, He'll call you by a nickname that speaks to who you are in the spirit realm.

When you hear Him, peace will steal into your room in the form of the Author and Perfecter of your faith, making the next silent stroke of His pen in your book of life. What is He writing in yours?

Ask.

Core Truth: We find healing when we come into resonant frequency with the Holy Spirit's sounds.

Let's Pray

Holy Spirit, I purpose to enter into the pulse of Your presence. I'm quietly listening for Your voice as I "livestream" You right now. What are You speaking into my soul? What is Your sound? My trust is found in You, Fulfiller of Promises. I purpose to match Your resonant frequency. What are You saying? What are You singing? I'm listening.

Take the Next Step

Where's your favorite place to be alone with Jesus, free of distraction? Set aside some time to settle in with Him there. Close your eyes. Ask the Holy Spirit to make you aware of His presence. What sounds do you hear? Write or draw what you sense.

---

[1]An excellent resource on seeing and hearing in the spirit is *4 Keys to Hearing God's Voice* by Mark and Patti Virkler.

Find Jesus in Your Painful Memory

Remain in me, as I also remain in you.

John 15:4

When I was a third-year college student, one beautiful fall afternoon I strapped on roller skates and took off down a hill. The dappled shadows of auburn oak trees and the smell of backyard barbecues filled me with energy. I soared down the sidewalk, feeling a rush of wind blowing my hair over my shoulders. But as I gained speed, I lost control. I grabbed a low-hanging branch over the sidewalk. *Snap!* The branch broke off in my hand.

Splat! I hit the pavement. My knees pounded with pain. I yanked off the skates and limped back to my dorm room in my stocking feet where I washed and bandaged my throbbing knees. Then I went back to the tree, tugged on one of its scrawny branches, and bounced it lightly. Was the risk I'd taken by speed skating the hill worth it? What was the experience trying to teach me?

Jesus Reveals His Role

When we hurt, where can we retreat to? It might sound unlikely, but sometimes revisiting the memory of a traumatic event is the safest place to go.

Our minds can be funny. After we experience the crisis of a trauma, later a similar situation can come up. When that happens, a similar pathway is triggered in our brains, and with it, fear—bringing back the original event to the memories in our minds and bodies.

Over the years, whenever the memory of the car accident with Ben flashed across the screen of my mind, I cringed. When I thought about the crush of the impact, I felt tension in my jaw and stomach. Anxiety sprang up without warning when police, ambulance, or fire truck sirens howled by. I felt waves of panic and migraines.

Weekly, I met with a counselor. She asked me to close my eyes and describe the memory of the accident.

I asked Jesus, "Where were You?"

It was July 1988, and I was on that all-too-familiar back road in Milpitas, California. I leaned over, pulled the rattle out of Baby Ben's hand, and I looked up in panic as the light pole came at us. *Crunch!* I heard and felt metal on metal as my car struck and flattened the light pole. My face and chest roared with pain. Ben howled, but I couldn't turn. My foot was bound by contorted floorboards. I felt powerless and terrified.

"God, help!" was all I could say.

In my mind, I whispered, "Jesus, where were You?" Then I went back to the memory and observed what He was doing.

I imagined Jesus standing by the light pole wearing

sunglasses, a bright T-shirt, shorts, and sandals on that hot July morning. He watched me take the rattle out of Ben's hand. He gave me the freedom to make a decision, for better or for worse. He was there *with* me. He was there *for* me.

He directed a man with a cell phone—rare in 1988—to drive down that side street, pull over, and call 911. Jesus prepared a squad of firemen, ready for action when their phone rang that morning. They arrived at the collision scene in minutes.

He sent a woman who had been shopping for steak to that road. She joined the quickly gathering crowd. When the paramedics showed up, they asked if anyone had ice in their car. She pulled the frozen steak out of a grocery bag. The paramedics applied the meat to the side of Ben's head to reduce the swelling. Jesus kept Ben awake—he never lost consciousness.

"Jesus, what are You thinking?" I asked.

"I'm right here. I haven't left. You made a mistake, but I don't condemn you. I'm here to help. *We're* going to help. See all these people I sent?"

"Yes, Jesus," I said, "But the pain is overwhelming. I can't do this."

"*You* can't," He agreed. "But together *we* can. Don't hold on so tight. Let go. I've got you covered."

I returned to my present-day conversation with Him.

"Jesus, what's the lie in that memory?"

"The lie is that because of a stupid decision, you're a terrible parent, a weak Christian, and a loser."

"Okay. What's the truth?"

"You made a bad judgment call. But you're a loving mother, a maturing disciple, and a winner. You're about to flip this around so I can use it for good."

"Okay. What comes next?"

"Go back into the memory."

So I did.

Jesus said, "Let's do an exchange. What do you want to give Me?"

"How about Ben's rattle? Ugh. I wish I'd never seen that thing."

"Great. Thanks. In exchange, here's a car key—for a new car. And another key to open doors of possibilities when you pray."

"Awesome, Jesus! Is there anything I need to apologize for?"

"You were speeding on that street. You broke the law."

"Hm. Jesus, You're right. I'm sorry for speeding."

"I forgive you. Do you see how you judged yourself?"

"Yeah, I did—thousands of times. I apologize."

"I forgive you for that, too."

Then silence. He raised an eyebrow and leaned forward, waiting for my response.

"Okay, Lord," I admitted softly. "I forgive myself."

Steps to Revisiting a Memory with Jesus

Do you want Christ to heal a painful memory? Take the following steps.

1. **Clear all distractions**. Turn off your electronics and shelve the "to do" list in your head. Be completely present with Christ. Quiet your soul. Don't be afraid of silence. If you don't hear anything at first, wait. Ask the Holy Spirit

to open your spiritual eyes and ears.

2. **Think back to the memory.** What were you thinking? Feeling?

3. **Ask God to search your heart.** What is the greatest point of pain? What did you struggle with the most? Give painful feelings permission to surface. Although this process hurts emotionally, you need to experience these feelings so that Jesus can heal them.

4. **Look for Jesus.** Where is He in the memory? Be open to creative images that come to mind. Maybe Jesus is wearing carpenter overalls and painting a fence, flying a kite, or climbing into a treehouse with you. Don't analyze or limit the image. Just go with it.

5. **Ask Jesus what He's thinking. What's He saying? What's He doing?** Imagine your dialogue. What do you ask? What's His reply? How does He respond to your pain? What is beyond your control? Is there anything that seems beyond His ability? What is truly in His power to do?

6. **Look for the lie.** When you see an event that triggered self-directed anger, ask Jesus if a lie is attached.

7. **Hand Him the lie as He gives you a God-truth.** What does the exchange look like? Be open to creative ideas. Are you exchanging a scooter for a mountain bike? A raft for a sailboat? A wrought iron fence for a pearl gate? A canary for an eagle?

8. **Ask Jesus to heal the memory.** Give over any sin to Him. Then accept His unconditional forgiveness. Forgive yourself. Be patient with the process.

9. **Open your Bible.** Ask the Holy Spirit for a Scripture to go with the experience. Record it.

10. **Share your impressions.** Talk to a mentor, counselor, or friend. What resonates with them? What do they confirm? What insights can they offer?

> When looking for Jesus in a memory, R.E.C.A.L.L.
> **R**emember the event and feelings.
> **E**xpect to see, hear, and sense Jesus.
> **C**onvert the lie to a God-truth.
> **A**ccept God's forgiveness.
> **L**et it go. Forgive yourself.
> **L**ook for a key Scripture and share your story with others.

When we ask Jesus, He'll point us back to the cross and tell us we've already been forgiven. He forgives us every time. *Every time.* Then we can worship Jesus and enjoy His peace. The tangible sense of His presence carries us, gives us rest, and grants us a sense of belonging.

Revisiting and Extending Trust

Years after my wipeout on roller skates, I went back to the memory. In my mind's eye, I stood on the sidewalk beside the brittle tree. I asked Jesus, "What do You see about my nature?"

He replied, "You were going too fast. Slow down. Don't get ahead of Me!" Then He smiled one of His funny crinkly-eyed smiles. "When things seem out of control, I'm with you and I see your needs. Be careful not to grasp at quick solutions. I've got it covered." And He leaned down, brushed off my knees, and gave me a gentle kiss. I felt a warm sensation flood my heart. Here was a Savior I could trust.

When you ask Jesus what He was up to in a memory, you gain His perspective. Will you forgive yourself? The response is up to you.

Core Truth: Focusing on Jesus' presence in our memories brings healing.

Let's Pray

Jesus, as I bring You my painful memory, increase my trust in Your goodness and kindness even when I can't see them. What was beyond my control? What seemed beyond Yours? Give me a sense of the truth about Your power. What divine exchange is available? Because I'm forgiven, no matter how harsh the circumstances seemed or how isolated I felt, I forgive and release myself. I worship You. Thank You for being my safe place.

Take the Next Step

Recall a painful memory. Take the steps in this chapter to focus on Jesus' presence in the memory. Give difficult emotions permission to surface. Where is Jesus in the memory? Make an exchange with Him. Take time to forgive yourself. Record any Scriptures that come to mind. Share your experience with a friend.

Healing: Bringing in the Five Senses

Beloved, I pray that in all respects you may prosper and be in good health, just as your soul prospers.

3 John 1:2 (NASB)

As I arrived at church one Sunday morning, two friends flagged me down in the foyer. "Here are a couple of books about healing. They're part of a series," one explained, thrusting them into my hands. "There are more in the bookstore."

I gave a tentative smile. "Thank you."

The truth was, I felt like a clumsy tennis player with a ball in one hand, a racquet in the other, and strands of a black net wrapped around me like the tentacles of an octopus. Defeat ridiculed me on the court. The words and actions of my friends, though well-intentioned, added to my conviction that others saw me in the same light.

Sometimes Words Aren't Enough for a Torn Heart

Carrying stormy memories of my childhood around in my head and heart, as an adult I asked others to pray off fear plenty of times. Well-meaning friends responded by filling my arms with stacks of reading material.

Though I diligently read the books, sometimes I overreacted when I couldn't anticipate what was about to happen. When coworkers spoke loudly or turned off lights in a room without warning, my heart pounded. A playful tap on my shoulder or tug of my sleeve startled me.

The slashes in my heart couldn't be stitched together with words.

Creation Fills Our Senses and Heals Us

To heal, I needed predictable experiences that filled my senses. In music classrooms, I was soothed by ripples of laughter from children and the cadence of their voices that rose and fell when they sang. The smell of cinnamon and nutmeg muffins warmed me. Hugs shored me up. When I woke in the morning, I smiled as the sun poured its golden hues through the branches of the pine trees in my yard, finger-painting patches of dappled sunlight across the lawn.

I enjoyed going on hikes on the sides of verdant Oregon mountains. There, I closed my eyes as lark and swallow songs serenaded my soul, and a warm breeze lifted the hair from my shoulders. Soft, burbling streams drew me. Each time I encountered flowing water, I paused to silently forgive those who'd hurt me. I took a reflective moment to forgive myself.

The Supernatural Blessing of Silence

As I opened up to close friends about my struggles, a couple of precious women drew wordlessly alongside, and we entered into the presence of our Comforter and Counselor together. They didn't judge me or overwhelm me with tons of words or literature. Like the Holy Spirit, they expected the best and gave me as much time as I needed. I learned to quiet my soul before God.

As I prayed, He often said, "My child, I love you." Sometimes He whispered in my heart, *"Be still, and know that I am God!"* (Psalm 46:10 NLT).

> There are no perfect days. Just imperfect days filled with God's perfect love.

In deep communion with Christ, I found my calm center. He accepted me just as I was and told me to accept myself, too.

In prayer, I came to know a supernatural world that existed beyond anything I could see, hear, or touch. I came to see the joy-crinkled face of Jesus and hear the soft timbre of His voice as he chuckled at my mishaps. I came to sense His presence when I needed courage.

Some days, the unseen world is more real to me than the seen world. I feel God's tangible presence. His mind and heart become mine—heaven on earth. Here is the peaceful place I need to calm my thoughts in order to forgive myself.

Friend, Christ loves it when you seek out times of His wordless joy. Where does His quiet presence reach you and offer serenity? That may be the best place to appropriate His grace for yourself, with or without words. You can always count on Jesus' compassion and acceptance. No matter the circumstances, you're a winner to Him.

I'm grateful that Christ loves us dearly—more than words can say.

Core Truth: Sometimes Christ heals us apart from words.

Let's Pray

Jesus, I open my heart to Your healing. Fill my eyes, ears, nose, hands, and heart with all of You. In the still, quiet hours, when words can't reach me, let Your deep, rich, and full peace permeate all of my mind and heart. Here I'm made complete in You. Here my soul prospers.

Take the Next Step

Take a break from journaling and settle in with pleasant sights, sounds, smells, textures, and tastes. Clear your mind of words that might crowd into this time. What sensations are you experiencing? Seeing? Hearing? Smelling? Feeling? Tasting? Connect with God without words, and relax in the simplicity of being in the moment with Him.

Section Five

Godly Perspective:
Take Back the Past

Trust That God Is in Control

Then he got into the boat and his disciples
followed him. Suddenly a furious storm
came up on the lake, so that the waves swept
over the boat. But Jesus was sleeping. The
disciples went and woke him, saying, "Lord,
save us! We're going to drown!"

Matthew 8:23–25

Following the car accident with Ben, I tried to make sense out of pain that an all-powerful God might have prevented. If I was going to drive my car off the side of the road and hop a curb, couldn't He have given me a small nudge to redirect me around the light pole and into the open field beside it? Maybe I didn't see the pole, but surely He did.

What's up with that?

When the Savior Seems to Miss His Wake-up Call

Sometimes our relationship with the Lord isn't what we expect. It seems like Jesus, who quieted the waves and filled burgeoning nets with fresh fish, can't reach us in our storm. Has He fallen asleep?

Picture this: you're riding out the storm of your worst, most humiliating moment. You're barely able to keep your head above the water as your body slams into the sides of the boat. You're smack-dab in the middle of icy, jarring, jaw-crunching waves. In the middle of the perfect storm, Jesus is sleeping peacefully in the back of the boat.

Do you think you should try to wake Him up? He's missing towering, terrifying sea swells throwing salt water into your eyes, tossing you around like popcorn.

Asleep. Jesus. *Creator* of the seas. This guy is way too calm.

He's clearly missing the action, oblivious that you're about to change the course of history with one *reeeally* bad move.

Doesn't Love Always Protect?

My daughter Emily is quiet, kind, and gentle. She's the kind of gal who never says a negative word. When she was five, I made fudge for the family, unaware that the butter I used was stale. Everyone but Emily wrinkled their noses after they took a bite. So I asked her, "On a scale of one to five, with five being the highest, what score do you give the fudge?"

She replied, "Six."

I brightened. "Wow, you like it that much?"

"Well," she said, "I couldn't find a number between one and five that I liked. So I gave it a six."

When she reached her twenties, sweet Emily told me that her middle school years had been the hardest ones of her life. At the private Christian school she attended, she was bullied. When the kids in her class saw how she struggled with academics, they turned their backs and called her names, saying she had a mental disability. They laughed and teased her.

The staff was no help. Her English teacher told her that she was slow, asked too many questions and wasn't paying attention. She told Emily that engaging with students a year younger showed that she couldn't relate to her peers.

When we spoke with the principal, he told us to persevere. He said that running away wouldn't solve the problem and dropping out of the school with just six months to go would only show defeat. Tim and I disagreed about what to do. He wanted to withdraw Emily from the school. I pushed back, insisting she finish out the year. So she did.

Eight years later, Emily told me she still had emotional scars from the experience. When I realized how hard that had been for her, tears streamed down my face. How could I have let such a tenderhearted kid stay in such a horrendous place?

I thought, "At the time, I figured I wanted to build strength in the battle. I wanted to show Emily the power of prayer. But look what that mistake cost her! Oh, and what about that verse from 1 Corinthians that says, '*Love always protects*'? So much for protecting my kid. I failed her in even that."

Then I shot up a prayer: "Lord, couldn't you have saved me from my own stupid mistake?"

You're Not the Only One with the Growth Curve

The Lord gently took me aside. He said, "That year, you were learning about your identity in Me. Maybe you didn't protect your daughter from harm. But I have already forgiven that. I saw your intent. Your heart was to persevere. When I look back, I see you with a greater compassion than you have for yourself. Join me in that compassion.

"You think you're the only one growing. Take another look. Emily is building her own story, a chapter at a time. What if I'm at work in her heart, teaching her how to forgive too?

"I'm in control. Know that the seeds of strife sown by those people haven't gone unnoticed. But they didn't take root in your daughter. She shook it off. That experience matured her."

In the Middle of Chaos: The Peace of Assurance

In the back of the boat, you stand over Jesus. Eyes closed, His head bounces on His chest to the rhythm of the sea swells.

And then: a holy moment.

You realize He's sleeping because He's one with heaven. Even as He rests, He's got absolute assurance that His Father's here. He gets it. He knows His Dad's in control.

Your Dad's in control.

And then you're filled with the sudden knowledge that when Jesus wakes up, He'll calmly assess the situation. He'll slay the vicious wind and relentless waves with authority-laden strength. Don't ask me how you know. You just know.

You just know *Him.*

And so you trust Him with your storm. No matter how much you lose, you know He'll redeem it. He'll bring peace and assurance that your Father is in control.

Now here is a Man you can rely on.

> *I regret days of strength to the extent that I relied on myself. I celebrate days of weakness, for then I relied on my Savior.*

Core Truth: We can rely on our Savior and His calming assurance.

Let's Pray

When storming thoughts of regret rage, deepen my trust in Your calm center. When memories and self-accusation keep me awake, I'll join You in living with our Father's peace. Calm my storm. Calm my memories. Calm *me.* I am one with Your breath, Your deep peace, and Your simple trust of a forgiving Father.

Take the Next Step

Think about a storm you've been through. Write a letter to your past self as you were experiencing the event, in the middle of the upheaval. What does the Holy Spirit show you about relying on Him in the chaos? Write a letter to Jesus about the outcome of the storm. What new truths is He revealing about His nature?

Can I Have a Do-Over?

My times are in Your hands.

Psalm 31:15

Imagine your life story on the big screen. Does a scene or two make you cringe? I've made thousands of trips to the theater of my mind and watched some scenes play and replay in infinite loops. I wished I could fire the executive producer, rip out massive sections of the story line, and roll out a better production. Cue the cameras and the clapboard.

But when I woke up from those daydreams, I had to face the results of my poor decisions. I had brought the consequences on myself and had no one else to blame.

The Volcano Blows

I've always loved words and have a passion for English and its fun peculiarities. So as a certified teacher, my dream job became teaching English as a Second Language. I was in a post-graduate ESL program with a perfect GPA. I served as a teaching assistant in the ESL department, teaching Latino,

Ukrainian, Romanian, and Asian children. I was certain I'd be offered a teaching position when one opened up. But I was in for a big surprise.

Mid-year, a job opening was posted for an ESL teaching job in the school where I worked. But I heard that the principal was considering a candidate for the job who had turned up in a random online search.

"What about the hard work I invested?" I thought. "Why consider anyone but me for the job?" I grew angry and blew my stack. I raised my voice in protest when I spoke with the vice principal. I complained loudly to another instructor without knowing the principal was within earshot.

The next thing I knew, the position was offered to the other teacher.

"I was such an idiot!" Tears streamed down my face as I realized all my hard work was like rainwater washing across the road, coursing into a gutter and down the sewer. Gone, just like that. And I had no one to blame but myself.

Head-smacking time.

If I could have a do-over, I'd swallow the angry words and unprofessional attitude. I'd lighten up a bit.

I went to the Master Storyteller Himself. I asked Jesus, "Hey, can I go back and do it over? I'd like to replay that scene."

Crickets.

"C'mon, Jesus," I pleaded. "Let's explore an alternate ending, like one of those *Choose Your Own Adventure* books!"

But He leaned forward and said, "I'm not giving back the rights to the story."

I thought for a good, long time, squirming. He knew the

beginning from the end. Surely He could see what went wrong. He's the all-powerful Producer, everywhere on the set at once, and determines how it all ends. Right?

"So, Jesus, You're saying I'm stuck with this? How do *You* see what happened? In fact, how do You see time?"

A Supernatural Perspective on Time

The Lord exists *in* time and *above* time. One of His nicknames is "God Who Sees"—meaning that He doesn't miss a thing that happens. He can open up a seat on a plane flight precisely when you need one. He's also called the "Ancient of Days," which means He can see the thread of time floating in the space of eternity *all at once*.

One of my favorite books, *Redeeming the Time* by Chuck Pierce, describes how God views temporal access. He reminds us that it's never too late to live the life of divine destiny.

"We have access to our past through the power of the Holy Spirit and the ability to set our course for the future. Consider, for a moment, the fact that God is not subject to the limitations imposed on us by linear time."[1]

Along the same lines, C.S. Lewis said this in *Mere Christianity:*

"God's life does not consist of moments following one another. If a million people are praying to Him at ten-thirty tonight, He need not listen to them all in that one little snippet which we call ten-thirty. Ten-thirty—and every other moment from the beginning of the world—is always the Present for Him. If you like to put it that way, He has all eternity in which to listen to the split second of prayer put up by a pilot as his plane crashes in flames."[2]

"Suppose God is outside and above the Time-line. In that case, what we call 'tomorrow' is visible to Him in just the same way as what we call 'today.' All the days are 'Now' for Him."[3]

He describes God's immediate access to all our lives—ongoing and continuous—past, present, and future. He says we can be forgiven for our past and redeem times that the enemy wanted to use against us.

Our brilliant Redeemer wants us to be wise as we view circumstances through His eyes. When we visit our past with regret, we're taking our eyes off Him. The Apostle Paul says that we need to walk with caution and wisdom, redeeming the time. We need to fall into step with our Redeemer, recognizing His ability to make things right. He says that God wants us to *"walk in wisdom toward them that are without, redeeming the time"* (Colossians 4:5 KJV). Pierce explains: "Redeeming the time refers to exercising wisdom as we recognize the times and seasons ordained by God for our lives."[4]

Sometimes the Lord takes us aside, puts His arm around our shoulders, and says, "Slow down. Take your time. I'm making a good thing of this. Believe me for it. I'm using this very circumstance to change you. Even when life seems irrational and the sense of timing is perplexing—especially then—My power and strength are transforming you. Will you search for My purposes here and now?"

Become a Possibilitarian

Those of us who activate possibilities with hope-filled expectation are called "possibilitarians." I love that word!

Possibilitarians see opportunities in *everything.* Jesus was the ultimate Possibilitarian.

When you enter my home, a colorful tapestry on the wall greets you with Christ's explosive *"With God all things are possible"* (Matthew 19:26). Jesus loves to show off His Father's wide-open opportunities.

> **As we begin to understand God's multi-dimensional nature, we can accept the past, because the ribbons of redemptive, crisscrossing possibilities intersect in us and our circumstances.**

Friend, no matter where you are today, you can get back on God's redemptive path for you. Perhaps you've taken a bypass off the freeway, but you'll ultimately get back on course if you look to Jesus. *"And we know that all things work together for good to those who love God, to those who are called according to His purpose"* (Romans 8:28 NKJV).

Trusting that God is with you in every moment is the key. Is God the God of second chances? Far more. He's the God of seven million chances—and beyond.

Throw Away the Timepiece

I've prayed one-on-one with thousands of people who have gone through job losses, prison terms, depression, financial ruin, divorce, and failed businesses. God released new beginnings for them. I knew the unwelcome intruder of regret, and I spoke to them about prevailing purposes they needed to uncover. I was amazed when simple prayers of

169

purpose opened up hope, a surge of self-acceptance, and access to an unseen world of power ironically gained through surrender.

When I was praying one morning, I held up an imaginary watch, clock, wall calendar, and smartphone calendar app before the Lord. I asked, "Will you reveal Your timeline in terms of minutes, hours, days, months, and years?"

He replied, "When you're in sync with Me, you can throw away the timepieces. I exist above the human concept of time."

Let God Define the Dream

Do you have unfulfilled dreams? I did. I wanted to be a full-time English teacher. But cycles of fibromyalgia prevented me from working full time in a classroom. I talked to my Healer. But the chronic pain persisted.

Every year, the school district put out an annual newspaper with an article announcing the Teacher of the Year. One spring afternoon, I opened my mailbox and turned the pages of the edition announcing that year's winner.

The teacher in the photo smiled. But I scrunched my face back at her.

"My picture should be over that caption." Heartsick, I crumpled up the newspaper. "What happened to my dream?" I asked God. "Where did I go wrong? Lord, You see events all at once. Why didn't You redirect me so that I could avoid all those years of pain and confusion?"

I didn't know how to interpret the silence that met me. For years, I needed to come to terms with letting go of anger with God. He told me that I was embracing a lie: that He and I were at cross purposes.

I told Him, "I don't get it. What do You have in mind?"

He replied, "I have another plan."

That plan took many years to understand. As a substitute teacher, I learned how to walk into a building and shift its atmosphere in a way that invited His presence and glorified Him. I entered crowded cafeterias and listened to people's stories. The Holy Spirit showed me how to discern students' spirits without relying on their outward appearance or academic achievement. On the playground, I spoke with children and searched for areas of giftedness to encourage and bless.

In the staff room, I listened to the other teachers' ongoing problems and gauged the spiritual climate so I could pray in sync with the Holy Spirit. I spoke Scripture over schools, sometimes walking up and down the hallways praying for students' and staff's hearts and minds to be filled with His presence. I released Jesus' promises in the classrooms, often allowing Christian students to linger on the topic of their faith in class discussions.

In training seminars, I prayed for revival to break out in the educational system. When I brought up God's name, I was often dismissed or ridiculed. At times, I felt I was contending alone, but the prayer warrior that those difficult years produced could not have been created without the staying power the process required. By God's grace, I rose above my circumstances and became tougher and more discerning along the way. Later, my articles about shifting atmospheres appeared in many publications.

God's timing, like His will, is good and pleasing and perfect.

Fast forward. I found my passion—God's forgiveness, the Holy Spirit's power, and our identity in Him—and I spoke about them in many venues. Was I teaching? Yes. But I had to surrender my definition of success to one on the Lord's terms.

All kinds of marvelous things happen when you give the Holy Spirit the job of shaping your dreams. Perhaps, at one time, you dreamt about having a close family. Maybe your biological family, or family by marriage, is no longer close—or never was. Who *has* Father God brought into your life instead? What would happen if you opened your heart to His definition of family for you?

When Success Seems to Tarry

I gain a tremendous amount of understanding about divine timing when I pray with intercessory teams. When business slowed for the software business Tim and I own, we had a prayer group join us at our office. They prayed for us and released God's promises over our company.

They read: *"Write the vision and make it plain on tablets, that he may run who reads it. For the vision is yet for an appointed time; but at the end it will speak, and it will not lie. Though it tarries, wait for it; because it will surely come, it will not tarry"* (Habakkuk 2:2–3 NKJV).

The paradox of that verse holds an unusual tension: *"Though it tarries, wait for it, because it will not tarry."* When I first heard those verses, the words didn't make sense. Though they're stalled, they're not stalling? A member of the prayer team saw an image of a car parked on a barge floating down the river—the vision of our potential for an appointed time. Then it dawned on me. Although we seemed to be making no progress with our business, God was, in fact, moving it forward.

Another member of the team saw an image of a UPS driver making deliveries across town with a package for us. Was he delayed? No. Although we were on his scheduled route, he was simply making a series of other deliveries before our stop. Then we were able to understand what God had in mind: if we understood that our need to wait was intentional, we could relax into His timing.

Friend, maybe you can't go back and do things over. But your Sovereign Producer regards your past scenes with a sense of supernatural purpose. When you get into step with Him, the desire to return to rewrite the past will dissolve as you reach forward for the screenplay of His favorite film—starring *you*. And in the process, you can watch trailers of coming features with eager expectation that fresh possibilities are rising.

Core Truth: In time and above it, God redeems our past and releases expansive, explosive possibilities.

Let's Pray

God, what's Your perspective from within time and above it? When I watch looping scenes of my life events, open my eyes so that I can see Your plan. On days when it seems like we're at cross purposes, deepen my awareness and trust that

You're working all things together for my good. Release fresh healing for my heart. I'm at peace with my past. Thank You!

Take the Next Step

If you could write a screenplay about a personal memory that has troubled you, what would you call it? Ask the Holy Spirit to touch your heart as you consider His dreams for you. What are the possibilities? If He were to produce a movie about your future, what would it be? Ask Him. Describe a two-minute trailer of that blockbuster movie.

---

[1]Chuck Pierce. *Redeeming the Time: Get Your Life Back on Track with the God of Second Opportunities*. Charisma House. 2009. pp. 90–91.

[2]C.S. Lewis. Mere Christianity. HarperCollins. 1980. p. 167.

[3]Ibid., p. 170.

[4]Pierce. p. 92.

Say "Thank You" 999 Times

In everything give thanks; for this is God's
will for you in Christ Jesus.

1 Thessalonians 5:18 (NASB)

My heart wants to be one with the Redeemer—a humble man who washed His disciples' feet. When I prayed, the Lord often told me I could become more like Him by humbling myself.

"Maybe an apology or two will do it," I thought. "And if one is good, then more is better, right?"

"Lord, I was speeding. I drove off the side of the road. My kid got a nasty head injury. *Gulp*. I'm sorry!"

"My son has a huge incision on the side of his head. I'm sorry!"

"Today he has an enormous headache. I'm sorry!"

"He has muscle spasms that twist his face to the side. I'm sorry!"

"I've lost my patience with him and yelled again. I'm sorry!"

Father God took me aside. "That's enough. Quit apologizing."

I asked, "What's the catch?"

"No catch. Just enjoy being forgiven."

"But wait!" I said. "Don't I need to make sure I've covered every bit?"

"No," He said, eyes sparkling. "You're asking forgiveness a thousand times. Repent once. Then return to the cross and say, 'Thank You' 999 times."

Our Big, Believable God

I'm a big fan of Bob Goff. In his book *Love Does*, he says he has learned to trust God and His forgiveness:

"When God is big enough and loves me enough to say He forgives me, I should actually believe Him. When I don't trust God's forgiveness, it's kind of like saying I really don't believe that He's good . . . I should stop asking God to forgive me over and over when He's made it clear He already has."[1]

Getting Personal with Jesus in Worship and Prayer

When we get stuck with self-directed resentment, maybe we need to get serious about warfare. Where does the best warfare take place?

When we're in an intense spiritual battle, author and speaker Graham Cooke says, we need to ask, "What level of worship does this call for?" Stepping into fresh, spontaneous worship brings restorative healing. I praised Father God for His goodness, even on days of intense pain.

Graham says, "Rejoicing and true thanksgiving produce peace and rest. That's because giving thanks from the heart will always overpower anything negative . . . Thanksgiving is not casual; it's an experience of the Lord's joy that liberates us to rejoice. Joy is the abiding atmosphere of Heaven, and so it changes our internal atmosphere permanently."[2] When I praised God in worship, I found my peace.

Along the way, I faltered when I saw others getting their healing, but I had no visible results. Graham taught me how to focus on process. I learned that the process is absolutely everything to the Lord—and the part He enjoys the most.

Over many years, I learned how to dispel negativity with grace. I declared war on negative emotions and allowed Holy Spirit joy to rise to the surface.

The world of the supernatural opened up expansive places of freedom. I enjoyed many joyful, forward-thinking God encounters as I prayed with others from an inward, renewed soul. I reveled in shared experiences with others who had crazy-supernatural Spirit encounters, too.

I learned the true essence of prayer—times of intimacy with Jesus. The more time I spent there, the more the Holy Spirit filled my senses, and I came to know Him more deeply. Graham Cooke taught me to look for "insteads." So instead of focusing on physical pain, I took inventory of my Heavenly Father's goodness. I discarded old patterns of lies, especially those of self-directed unforgiveness and resentment, and instead, declared fresh, future-present understanding of my Christ-identity. I was able to forgive myself and release bitterness. I found upgrade after upgrade in my thoughts, actions, and words.

Over the years, I heard stories about God's kindness released in healing as people persisted in prayer. In the person of the Holy Spirit, I found the courage and strength to persevere. He pointed me to a confidence found in the person of Jesus Christ, the Fulfiller of Promises.

Graham Cooke invites us to consider our upgrades. In *The Nature of God,* he says, "The question shouldn't be, 'Why is this happening to me?' The 'why' question is never answered on earth. It is the wrong question. It should be, 'What is it that God wants to be for me now that He couldn't be at any other time, in any other way?' What is it about your current situation that is designed to bring you into a deeper relationship with God?"[3] When you ask that, be prepared for extraordinary answers!

> *Focus on appreciation . . . can change heart rhythm patterns from chaotic to smooth and rhythmic, like ocean waves.[4]*

A deep, relational place with God the Father, the Source of renewed vision, is not a temporary resting place. We are called to live there—and to embrace the process that He uses to renew our minds as we shed layers of perceived limits. Then we can boldly take our expression of His glory to the next level.

Core Truth: We can repent once and thank Christ 999 times.

Let's Pray

Jesus, I pray from a place of Your renewal in my soul. I commit to a deeper relationship with You. My confidence is found in You alone. After repenting—thinking differently about my past—I thank You for Your forgiveness 999 times!

Take the Next Step

In your journal, write a letter to Jesus, thanking Him for His forgiveness. How does gratitude impact your self-forgiveness journey?

---

[1]Bob Goff. *Love Does: Discover a Secretly Incredible Life in an Ordinary World.* Thomas Nelson. 2012. p. 124.

[2]http://brilliantperspectives.com/god-will-not-let-stay-stuck/ (Retrieved October 7, 2016.)

[3]Graham Cooke. *The Nature of God: Upgrading Your Image of God and Who He Wants to Be for You.* Brilliant Book House. 2003. p 22.

[4]http://www2.heartmath.org/webmail/17232/370231396/ cf370f9612f302c94d3b6604c26aa8ea311a44370f0ed43d191072b98e99 f463 Sara Childre, President, HeartMath Institute. (Retrieved September 21, 2016.)

The Magic of Reverse:
Take 3 Steps Back

For my thoughts are not your thoughts,
neither are your ways my ways, declares the
LORD.

Isaiah 55:8

My doctor tells me that instead of moving forward, I need to take a couple of steps back.

For years, Dr. Robert Allen (fondly known as Dr. Bob), a chiropractor in Vancouver, Washington, served athletes in the Olympics, the NBA, PGA, and NASCAR. He was intrigued that in their training, many ran backward. When he asked the athletes and their coaches why, they couldn't explain. As he observed patients in his regular practice who suffered with locked-up vertebrae, he thought about the athletes and resolved to discover more about the reverse stride.

Measuring 100 patients' backward steps, Dr. Bob tested differences in their muscle group strength. With the first and second steps, there was no change. But then he made an amazing discovery: on the third step backward, the muscle groups suddenly came into alignment.[1]

What happened? The previously torqued spine unwound, like the release of a stretched, twisted rubber band. *Joomp!* The tension was released, their bodies responded, and they began to heal.

Dr. Bob tells patients, "I had a '79 four-wheel drive Chevy truck. To get it out of four-wheel drive, I had to drive backward—then it came unlocked. It had to unwind the general torque. Our spines are like that."

The Bigger Picture Is Right Back There

Backward steps don't just help our spines unwind. They also help us gain a clearer perspective.

Dr. Bob lives on a ranch. "I ride my horses in the back country where there are no trails. Periodically, I'll take an orange flag and put it on a tree. After I cross a road, sometimes I'll turn around and go back a little bit to get my bearings. Once I see where I've been, I can tell where I'm going and take a new look.

> In life, we tend to think we have to step forward all the time. It's good to take a couple of steps back.
> ~ Dr. Robert Allen, DC

"The key is that you have a completely different picture. When you're blazing through, you don't have the vision. It's more tunnel vision of 'this is where I need to get,' or 'this is the easiest way for me to go, because of how the trees are down, or the brush is thicker.' But if you step back from it, you can see the whole picture—

the greater purpose."[2]

When you and I look over our shoulders, sometimes we feel that instead of making progress, we have actually regressed. We act out of immaturity. We see symptoms we thought we'd put behind us. "Grrr. I thought I was over that!"

Father God honors our quest for understanding when we come to Him and ask, "What do You perceive here? What are You thinking?"

I focus on emptying myself in my quiet times. God already has a brilliant plan, so I come gently before Him and ask, "What are You up to? I come into agreement with that."

What if the Holy Spirit, our athletic Coach, says, "Here you go. Put it in reverse. Back up and tell me what you see"?

We might confess, "All I see in my past are my shortcomings. Am I destroying Your plan?"

His response might surprise us.

Relaxing into a Greater Purpose

Taking three steps back might provide a chance for us to enter into a new sense of God-ordained authority we never dared carry before. As we look at our circumstances, we can dialogue with God, even when He's downright irrational. We usually crave the certainty we need to move forward boldly, but we are sometimes wound up with insecurity because of setbacks.

When it seems we are traveling backward, Jesus might be giving us the chance to relax our tense and twisted outlooks, just like walking backward relaxes our spines.

> **What are you discovering about yourself as you continue to practice self-forgiveness? How have you changed? What is your heart like now? Are you more loving toward yourself? More loving toward others?**[3]
> ~ Dr. Robert Enright

Sometimes we'll see a greater purpose—His. And when we don't really get it, that's okay, too. Because when *"we do not know how to pray as we should, the Spirit Himself intercedes for us with groanings too deep for words; and He who searches the hearts knows what the mind of the Spirit is, because He intercedes for the saints according to the will of God"* (Romans 8:26–27 NASB).

You can trust that the Holy Spirit is speaking to your Heavenly Father on your behalf. He's got His bearings. He sees where you've been. He knows where you're going. All you need to do is trust and follow Him.

Core Truth: We recalibrate by taking three steps back and gaining God's point of view.

Let's Pray

Holy Spirit, as I take three steps back, I seek clarity gained with Your broader perspective. I rejoice in the mercy You have shown me, the favor that has surrounded me, and the grace that empowers me to accomplish what You set before me. Thank You for steadying me as I grow.

Take the Next Step

Take two photos. In the first, zoom in closely on the flaw of a single feature of a building, like a scratched door knob, dirty window, or debris-covered roof. For the second photo, zoom way back. What do you notice about that feature of the house with the new perspective?

Visit a painful memory. Take three steps back and view it with God-centric eyes. What do you see? What "pops"?

---

[1]Dr. Robert Allen. Personal interview. October 29, 2010.

[2]Ibid.

[3]Dr. Robert Enright. *8 Keys to Forgiveness.* W. W. Norton and Company. 2015. p. 191.

When God Gives You
a New Nickname

Do not fear, for I have redeemed you;
I have called you by name; you are Mine!
Isaiah 43:1 (NASB)

"What does your name mean?" I often ask people when I meet them for the first time. I'm amazed that most say they don't know. When we call folks by their names, we are speaking out their identity. Sarah: Princess. Jessica: God beholds. Kathryn: Pure, clear. Susan: Lily. Elizabeth: Oath of God. Lynn: Waterfall. Ryan: Little King. Joe: May God give increase. Robert: Bright. Ben: Son of My right hand. Christopher: Carrier of Christ. Michael: Who is like God?

I have some pretty funny nicknames. When I have 26 projects going at once, I call myself the A to Z Girl. Searching out business prospects earned me the name Bird Dog. And the ability to gauge elapsed time without looking at a clock inspired my family to call me Mrs. Chronometer.

Over the years, Tim and I have named our cars Alice, Cuisse, Roo, Iced Tea, and Google. We call our wild hummingbird Dinkle Tinklemeyer ("Dinkie" for short). What are some nicknames in your world?

A Nickname for Every Trial

As I connected with the Holy Spirit over the years, I began to develop a curiosity about what God might call me.

A few years ago, at a summer writing conference, I promised a friend a ride home. But just as we were getting ready to leave, I lost my keys. In waves of sweltering 102-degree heat, I retraced my steps, going in circles and fighting tears of frustration.

"I lose things all the time," I thought to myself. "That makes me a loser."

My mind swept through the messages we'd just heard at the conference. One of the keynoters had challenged us to ask God for a new nickname—a new identity to call our own.

So I prayed. In my mind's eye, Jesus laughed, took me by the hand and led me into a council room where He, Father God, and the Holy Spirit held a round-table discussion.

"Do you see how Lynn lost her keys? She's persisting in her search and until they show up. She makes sweeps and finds things."

The Lord turned to me and grinned. "I call you Finder."

"You call me *Finder*?" I asked, shaking my head with disbelief.

I repeated it to myself. "He calls me Finder."

I returned my focus to the search. I leaned inside my car and found the keys right where I had left them—in the ignition. I drove my friend home, offering apologies for the delay.

Suddenly I caught on. If God was calling me Finder, then I must be an ace at finding things. Parking spaces opened up. At networking events, I found strategic business partners. When I met up with people who needed a word of encouragement specific to a crisis, I found Bible verses. And I was often the last to leave events, because I lingered to pray with people, finding Kingdom gold in them and sharing what I saw in their hearts.

I started a list on an electronic app. I wrote, "I am Finder. I find hidden treasures and purpose in adversity with ease. *"Seek and you will find"* (Luke 11:9). I prayed, "Lord, open my ears, so I can learn Your new nicknames for me!" I became excited when He opened my ears—and spiritual eyes—to fresh identities rising up in me.

I hungered for leaders to see the arrival of God's answers to our prayers. He called me Rhoda, the servant girl in Acts 12 who announced the miracle of Peter's prison escape in response to the prayers of Mary and her friends. I added to my new list, "I am Rhoda. I hear knocking at the door and announce the arrival of miracles. 'Mary, it's Peter! Peter's at the door!'"

When I had conflicts with Tim, and realized I was taking things too seriously, I listened for God's voice. I heard Him whisper in my heart, "I love it when you release joy!"

So I added another nickname to my list. "I am Joy-Starter. I release joy, the threaded needle that stitches together heaven and earth. With my laughter, I release delight, wonder, and permission to lighten up. I laugh when the enemy's lies are exposed. As others chime in, lies dissolve."

When I connected with business owners and their

employees, I encountered sectors of our city who'd lost hope. I purposed to pray, "Draw me to where you're already at work, Lord." After networking events, I followed up with contacts over coffee. I encouraged them, maybe not with chapter and verse, but with warm smiles and words of appreciation. I prayed, "Holy Spirit, illuminate my next step." Sometimes, that next step was an email, phone call or encouraging note in the mail.

When I prayed, in my mind's eye, I saw Jesus smiling and pointing to the roof of my home. He said, "You are Fiddler on the Roof. You're releasing a melody across town as you encourage people." I fancied myself climbing onto rooftops and intentionally shifting atmospheres. There Christ's love filled the air waves with kindness and encouragement, rolling across to others in my city.

New Battle, New Name

I keep a special journal with my nicknames. I designate several pages for each, including a Scripture verse and fun pictures. I continue to add new nicknames when I go through tough times.

I have become very familiar with those names. Now, as I approach the Lord in prayer, I ask, "Father, who do You call me?" The dialogue and journal entries that follow are filled with God-winks.

What if every time you go through an experience and deal with overwhelming heartache, God sees your true identity and gives you a new name? For example, did you experience a big financial loss? Maybe He calls you Investor. Did a relationship go south? For sure, He calls you

Friend. Did you plant seeds that seemed to sprout only thorns? I'll bet He calls you Rose.

Friend, when you hear God's new names for you, write them down and find Scriptures and images to go with them. Journaling about God-encounters that open up when He calls you by your new name can be uplifting. I invite you to share your experience with others so they can have a go of it, too.

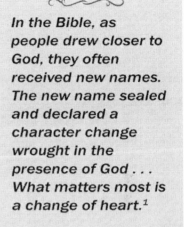

In the Bible, as people drew closer to God, they often received new names. The new name sealed and declared a character change wrought in the presence of God . . . What matters most is a change of heart.[1]

What new nickname is God giving you today?

Core Truth: No matter what others call us, God's names for us reveal our strengths and virtues.

Let's Pray

God, who do You call me? I trust Your names for me, regardless of what came before or follows. I choose to echo the identity You release there. You are the One Who Accepts Like No Other.

Take the Next Step

On a journal page, name a crisis you have experienced. What was the biggest point of pain, such as fear, grief, or injustice?

Ask Father God to help you name the opposite quality, such as peace, joy, or justice. Ask Him for a nickname based on the positives He sees in you.

Draw the nickname with jumbo doodle letters and decorate it with images that go with it. For example, someone experiencing rejection might sense God calling her "Treasure." Images on the bubble letters of "Treasure" might be a compass, shovel, gold, diamonds, rubies, sapphires, necklaces, and rings. Be creative. Beneath the nickname write a Scripture verse to go with it.

---

[1]John Avery. *The Name Quest: Explore the Names of God to Grow in Faith and Get to Know Him Better.* Morgan James Publishing. 2015. p. 15.

Ask Fresh Spirit-Led Questions

Dear friends, if our hearts do not condemn us, we have confidence before God and receive from him anything we ask.

1 John 3:21–22

It was 5:30 on a clear-as-blue-glass-sky June morning. Children of all ages showed up to enjoy hot air balloons preparing to launch at the Tigard, Oregon Festival of Balloons.

Men worked hard to steady the sturdy ropes—tethers that anchored the balloons to the earth. But not for long. Inside the vehicles, propane burners fired up, whispering, "Ascent! Ascent!" Excitement mounted in the crowd spread across the huge open field.

Then the 212-degree air inside the balloons lifted them into 2,000-foot arcs above the crowd, opening a doorway to heaven adorned in a miraculous double halo rainbow that stretched across the firmament. Young kids tilted their heads back, pointing to the balloons—or was it the rainbows? Maybe both.

Soon 17 red, yellow, orange, blue, purple, green, and gold orbs lit up the morning sky. The sun eased up and over the horizon.

Our journey of self-forgiveness is a wondrous hot air balloon ride. When we release tethers of lies and cut ourselves free from hindrances keeping us down, we become buoyant with a warmer attitude of kindness and acceptance.

Along the way, the Holy Spirit will likely direct our attention to the flames He's lit. His fire—the glory of God within us—rises, soars, and sweeps us to new places in the supernatural. He says, "Get over it! Get above your circumstances and view them from heaven to earth." He coaxes us to swap out our limited feet-on-the-ground view of circumstances for a ride that affords us a powerful, expansive vantage point from above.

When we're tempted to be discouraged, we can reframe the situation by praying, "Holy Spirit, what's going on? How must I shift my thinking to see what You see?" Then, with His upward lift, we can reach forward from a whole new world.

Taking Questions to the Next Level

For years, I asked God, "Why did you allow me to go through a car accident with my son?" Then, 25 years later, I was in another terrible collision, resulting in a nasty head and neck injury. I saw a number of specialists, including chiropractors, counselors, and physical therapists, who gradually helped me get back on my feet.

I found that each professional had their own set of questions: "What's the level of pain in your back? What is your range of motion? How are you progressing on your stretches and exercises? Are you pacing yourself?"

I realized that the Holy Spirit was part of my team. I asked Him how He might shape my mind and heart. He told me to ratchet up our relationship by posing different kinds of questions.

The Holy Spirit loves inquiring minds. He enjoys hanging out with us and doesn't mind unresolved issues. He understands that we're growing, and He cheers us on even when our growth can't be charted with a straight line.

Consider these questions:

- *What are You releasing in me?* Releasing can mean eliminating, like releasing fear, or depositing, like releasing hope.

- *Holy Spirit, where's the good that I haven't yet seen?* If God is good all the time, and we wrestle with the evil in a situation or memory, then we can ask for a revelation of His goodness.

- *Lord, when I call on You, which name do I use?* One of my favorite books is *The Name Quest* by John Avery. I found out that the Lord has more than 500 names. He wants us to become familiar with many and use them to deepen our relationship with Him.

  Almighty God. The God of Abraham, Isaac, and Jacob. Comforter. Counselor. Compassionate God. Lovingkindness. God Almighty. Lamp. The Lord Who Heals You. Messenger of the Covenant. Bridegroom. Best Friend. Champion. When we call Him by name, our expectancy for His power rises, and our relationship with Him deepens.

- *How can I be more open to the ways You fill my senses?* When we intentionally live in the present, we can relax and be more receptive to His thoughts.

- *How is Your love changing me?*

- *How are You renewing me? What part of the process is Yours to renew? Which part is mine?*

- *What do I need to forgive myself for?*

- *What do I need to forgive others for? Where are there unresolved conflicts? Do I need to humble myself, take responsibility, and make amends?*

- *What do I need to forgive You for? In what area do I need to trust You more?*

- *What is shifting in my sense of authority? What can I do to reinforce it?*

- *Here's a blank page in my book of life. What are You writing?*

- *Do You want me to stay in this place—neighborhood, job, geographical location? Or should I move? If so, when should I make the move?*

- *What fruit are You growing most in me: love, joy, peace, patience, kindness, goodness, faithfulness, gentleness, or self-control? What evidences of that fruit do You see in me?*

- *Is there a creative way of looking at this? What do You find good-natured or funny about this situation?*

- *Which of Your resources for this situation seem limited but are really endless? You are the God of limitless resources. Am I praying too narrowly—and limiting my results?*

- *What are these circumstances preparing me for?*

- *What relationships are You building? Is there a new dream? And with it a new team?*

Seeking Heaven's Counsel

Asking questions opens up a dialogue with the Holy Spirit that takes us into a deeper relationship with Him. Our confidence isn't found so much in knowledge as in the person of the Holy Spirit Himself. We worship. We settle in with Him. We ask. We worship

> **Sometimes we don't have the answers. All we need is Spirit-led questions.**

some more. We relax, leaving the outcome to Him.

Then we wait expectantly for Him to answer with the wisdom of His counsel. *"Nevertheless I am continually with You; You have taken hold of my right hand. With Your counsel You will guide me, and afterward receive me to glory. Whom have I in heaven but You? And besides You, I desire nothing on earth"* (Psalm 73:23–25 NASB). Our Comforter and Counselor promises to see us through tough times when we make space for Him.

When our questions show that all we desire is more of God's glory, He fulfills that desire. Because we are God's children, He accepts our questions. He knows that we want to understand His nature better. *"I am writing to you, little children, because your sins have been forgiven you for His name's sake"* (1 John 2:12 NASB). As a natural act of Fatherly love, God forgives our sins. And we, His children, trust His grace because we trust *Him.*

Core Truth: Asking the Holy Spirit fresh questions deepens our relationship with Him.

Let's Pray

Holy Spirit, upgrade my questions so that my purposes align with Yours. When I don't find the answers I'm looking for, I trust that simply wanting more of You is enough. What new question can I ask in this situation?

Take the Next Step

In your journal, write three new questions for the Holy Spirit. Listen for the answers. Write His responses, which may come in the form of more questions. What is He revealing about His nature?

Section Six

Overcoming:
Taste Victory

The Explosive Freedoms
of Self-Forgiveness

*Stand fast therefore in the liberty by which
Christ has made us free, and do not be
entangled again with a yoke of bondage.*
Galatians 5:1 (NKJV)

When we forgive ourselves, we gain freedom at many levels. Because the Holy Spirit lives within us, His unbridled moves are ours too.

Realizing the newfound freedoms that come with a burst of self-acceptance can feel like dynamite has suddenly blasted open the doors of your prison cell, releasing you from bondage. The power of self-forgiveness is downright explosive!

Consider these freedoms that result when we forgive ourselves.

Freedom from Regret

"Forgetting what lies behind and reaching forward to what lies ahead, I press on toward the goal for the prize of the

upward call of God in Christ Jesus" (Philippians 3:13–14 NASB). When we let go of our past, we reach forward and upward into our calling more richly and fully. Our natural talents and spiritual gifts are released and we live out our Kingdom assignments as sons and daughters of the Most High God.

Among the nicknames the Lord has given me, my favorite used to be Regret Shredder. When I looked at my past, any time I felt regret, I was certain the Lord wanted me to shred it to bits. He blessed those scraps and slices. I was happy to see it reduced to ribbons.

But then, two years later, he told me that name wasn't mine. I heard Him say, "An even better landscape awaits you—the No-Regret Zone. That's where I want you to go. That's where I want you to live. Contend for this territory. Confident of My power, don't look back."

Friend, I invite you to shred any regret you have for the past. Let it go! Then join me in the No-Regret Zone. Here Truth thrives. The ground pulses with His life!

Freedom from Self-Judgment

"Therefore do not pronounce judgment before the time, before the Lord comes, who will bring to light the things now hidden in darkness and will disclose the purposes of the heart. Then each one will receive his commendation from God" (1 Corinthians 4:5 ESV). When we give over the rightful place to the Judge and accept His forgiveness, we walk free.

When my kids were young and disobeyed, I sometimes yelled at them. My angry words and harsh tones were anything but kind.

It wasn't until they were much older that I recognized that I had been angry with myself and had taken it out on them. When I spoke with my Comforter and Counselor, the Holy Spirit, He told me that my Heavenly Father had it covered through His Son's sacrifice. The judgment was complete. I was free. I was forgiven. With His acceptance, I slowly learned to accept myself.

Freedom from Fear and Anxiety for the Future

"Do not be anxious about anything, but in everything, by prayer and petition, with thanksgiving, present your requests to God. And the peace of God, which surpasses all understanding, will guard your hearts and your minds in Christ Jesus" (Philippians 4:6–7).

When we say, "Thank You" to the Lord, He inhabits the praise of His people (see Psalm 22:3). And when He inhabits us, His peace governs our hearts and minds.

I used to think that wildly successful people had no problems in their lives. They relaxed into every situation and nothing bad ever happened to them, right? What did they know about freedom? They were born that way.

As I hung around those people and got to know them, I realized they had just as many challenges as the rest of us. They had conflicts with their families. They had disputes over money. They got headaches. They had time management issues.

Then I recognized the difference: they made a conscious choice to focus on what they had the power to change. They realized that their attitudes were conscious decisions that propelled their next actions. And each action was a functional value statement that showed where their heart was. They gave over to God what belonged to Him.

I thought to myself, "That's what I want to do. I'm going to let God highlight His choices for me. I'll take the best and leave the rest."

When I had conflicts with my family, I chose to acknowledge their points of view. When I disagreed with Tim about budget decisions, I asked the Holy Spirit how to frame my conversations with him. When I got headaches, I took breaks to relax and stretch my muscles. When I scrambled to get on top of time management, I asked the Holy Spirit for wisdom.

Freedom to Hear the Holy Spirit's Sound

> *Where the Spirit of the Lord is, there is freedom.*
> *2 Corinthians 3:17 ESV*

Freedom showed up in a surprising way: the more I surrendered the outcome of an issue to God, the more relaxed I became. And the more relaxed I was, the easier it was to hear the Holy Spirit's sound.

For a couple of years, I was a member of Graham Cooke's international prayer organization, The Warrior Class. I was on a team called the Freedom Fighters. When problems came up, I considered each unwelcome restraint. I wrote in big letters on the white board in my home, "How would a Freedom Fighter frame it?"

I shook off attacks of the enemy with the help of friends

who prayed. Sometimes, stress brought past trauma—like the car accidents or childhood storms—to the surface, and I overreacted. When I blew it, I asked the Holy Spirit to remind me what freedom sounded like.

I heard a soft hush, the sound of silence—a blank space, free from haste and frenzy. The clanging of a bell in a bell tower declared liberty. Melodies of freedom filled my heart and mind. Rushing water reminded me of His presence. Rivers, streams, and breakers splashed to remind me to restore, to reconcile, and to surrender to God that which belonged to Him.

Freedom to Express Creativity

"Whatever you do, work heartily, as for the Lord and not for men, knowing that from the Lord you will receive the inheritance as your reward. You are serving the Lord Christ" (Colossians 3:23–24 ESV). When we tackle projects, we can relax into mistakes we make along the way, because Holy Spirit creativity lives within us. We don't have to approach things the way others do or even the way we've done them in the past.

What is He calling you to create? Do you write? Paint? Dance? Bake? Tell stories? Raise kids? Teach? Develop computer code? Something that's never been done before? Serve Christ creatively.

Freedom to Relax and Enjoy the Present

"Therefore I tell you, do not worry about your life, what you will eat or drink; or about your body, what you will wear . . .

But seek first the kingdom of God and his righteousness, and all these things will be given to you as well" (Matthew 6:25,33).

When you focus on your righteousness—that is, being morally right with God—you don't need to worry. You can relax into His provision and enjoy whatever you are experiencing in the present moment. He'll meet you right where you are, no matter how much or how little you've accomplished.

Freedom to Rest

"But when you go over the Jordan and live in the land that the LORD your God is giving you to inherit . . . he gives you rest from all your enemies around, so that you live in safety" (Deuteronomy 12:10–11 ESV).

When we forgive ourselves, we step into our inheritance, and we find rest from the enemy. Imagine on a lazy afternoon, you are stretched out on a hammock, at complete peace, breathing slowly and evenly. Your heart beats in cadence with Jesus' pulse.

When the enemy comes at you, his attack is sliced to ribbons on the tree-tied hammock strings. Here restful peace does vengeance. We have freedom from anxiety and strife when we rest. The place of self-directed mercy is a safety zone.

Freedom from Self-Centeredness

"Praise be to the God and Father of our Lord Jesus Christ, the Father of compassion and the God of all comfort, who

comforts us in all our troubles, so that we can comfort those in any trouble with the comfort we ourselves receive from God" (2 Corinthians 1:3–4).

I lost a baby girl to stillbirth in 1991. Little Mary Beth turned over and over in one direction, twisting her umbilical cord and cutting off her source of nutrition. The anguish of quiet nights and empty arms was overwhelming. Not many people understood. I journaled about the experience. One day, I reached out and shared a poem about Mary Beth called *Still.* A hospital chaplain who ministers to parents with infant loss picked up the poem, which is used today to comfort and steady broken hearts.

We gain a deeper understanding of Holy Spirit counsel when we extend God's comfort to ourselves. When we extend it to others, we take it one step further and change a community.

Freedom to Worship Unrestrained

"Come, let us bow down in worship, let us kneel before the LORD *our Maker"* (Psalm 95:6). When our minds are free from condemnation, our arms are open wide, welcoming our Redeemer's transforming presence. He changes us from the inside out.

When David moved the Ark of God to Jerusalem, he stepped into God's complete favor by worshiping with all his might. The Israelites shouted and sounded a trumpet. He said, *"I will play music before the* LORD. *And I will be even more undignified than this, and will be humble in my own sight"* (2 Samuel 6:21–22 NKJV).

Worship is the place of God's complete acceptance.

Freedom from Envy

"A heart at peace gives life to the body, but envy rots the bones" (Proverbs 14:30).

Envy says that what others have is better than what we've got. That dissatisfaction is the sign of a lie that says God our Provider has not blessed us with enough.

When our souls are quiet before Him, though, we can choose gratitude for who He is and who He's becoming for us. We gain a peace about who we are and who we're becoming for Him. We no longer have room to compare ourselves to others or to come up short. A place of self-acceptance says, "I've settled in with my identity in Jesus. His grace is more than enough for me."

> As Christ sets you free, leap and grab hold of the bell tower rope, hang on by its tail end, and swing and clang for all you're worth.

Friend, when we forgive ourselves, the unrestrained place of openness and joy is worth everything we've surrendered. And in the process, we'll find a newfound ability to speak to ourselves with broader and greater patience.

Core Truth: When we forgive ourselves, we gain expansive freedom.

Let's Pray

Holy Spirit, I'm free from self-judgment, fear, and anxiety, because I'm filled with Your resurrection power. You have not given me the spirit of fear, *"but of power, and of love, and of a sound mind"* (2 Timothy 1:7). I welcome fresh waves of Your creativity. I relax in You. Who can I share my gifts with? I'm venturing out to the landscape called the No Regret Zone with You. I worship You in Spirit and in truth.

Take the Next Step

What's your favorite song about freedom or a song that makes you feel free? Rewrite the lyrics to make it about Holy Spirit freedom. Share it with a friend.

The Object of the Game: Overcome!

For everyone who has been born of God
overcomes the world. And this is the victory
that has overcome the world—our faith.

1 John 5:4 (ESV)

A couple of years ago, following a writers' conference where I'd served on the leadership team, the needle on my stress-o-meter spiked into the red zone. I needed to blow off steam.

Tim and I drove two hours to Pacific City, Oregon. As we walked the gusty beach, I chatted on a conference call with a few Freedom Fighters. Suddenly, a looming sneaker wave appeared out of nowhere. Frightened, I pivoted fast but tripped across tire tracks in the sand, twisted, and fell hard onto my side. A butcher's knife of pain slashed my shoulder.

The spill separated my collarbone from the sternum. For months, relentless, excruciating pain pierced me with every motion. Sleep evaded me. Friends prayed, but progress was slow. I needed to renew my mind. But how?

When the World Is Looking for a Fight

Have you ever been injured in a fall that made you feel beat up? Or have you had a bad falling-out with a friend? A fight is a fight.

Maybe you're living with a family member or dealing with a coworker whose choices are a source of ongoing anguish. No matter the reason, it's easy to fall into a victim mentality. "Well, they started it!"

As I write this chapter, I'm having a terrible, horrible, no-good, very-bad week. I erased two years of audio files on my phone. The windshield of my car leaked, and it rained inside the passenger compartment, disabling my garage door opener. A remodeling project in my kitchen kicked up brick dust and sawdust that went everywhere, and I fought debilitating headaches. An oppressive spirit weighed me down, leaving me in tears. I felt like the world was ganging up on me. *Aargh!*

The Squeeze Factor

I find that when I'm tired and frustrated with too many factors beyond my control, I turn my frustration and anger inward. I think, "What did I do wrong?" I feel under condemnation when I battle a heavy spirit like that.

Jesus said, *"These things I have spoken to you, that in Me you may have peace. In the world you will have tribulation; but be of good cheer. I have overcome the world"* (John 16:33 NKJV). The word "tribulation" means "pressure, oppression, crushing, squashing, or squeezing."[1] When olives or grapes are squeezed in a press, they go through a great deal of pressure. We feel this same kind of crunch when the squeeze of circumstances comes from all sides. Jesus told us to expect this feeling: "You will have tribulation."

When I'm in tears for weeks, I know I'm taking life entirely too seriously. It's time to lighten up and get my head back in the game.

Every Game Has an Object

Do you like good-natured competition? When I was a kid, my friends and I played board games for hours. Whenever we discovered a new one, we looked over the rules to determine the object of the game. Maybe the winner wound up with the most money. Or the most cards. Or the most points.

What if every trial had a divine "object of the game"? What would it be?

The object of the game is to move as quickly as possible from a victim mindset to that of an overcomer. Put victory into motion, declaring it rapidly. You have already won!

When we develop a relationship with God who sees everything and is present everywhere, we can refuse a victim stance. *"Who is he who overcomes the world, but he who believes that Jesus is the Son of God?"* (1 John 5:5 NKJV). To "overcome" is to "come over" the circumstances with heaven's multi-dimensional view.

When I ask God for His perspective, in my mind's eye I often see something like a screen playing a movie scene. For instance, when my kitchen was being remodeled, pots, pans, dishes, and bowls stored in boxes were covered with brick dust. As I prayed, I envisioned the completed kitchen. Through tears, I thanked Him out loud for the new cupboards, oven, and floor. God sees forward. I spoke it out with the understanding that He'd fill in what was necessary to get there.

Picture yourself in the future, holding up a trophy, and then bring it back to the present. Lost your confidence? Declare, "Lord, maybe I can't see it yet, but we're going to take this win to the next level."

"Now faith is confidence in what we hope for and assurance about what we do not see" (Hebrews 11:1). Faith is belief in the trophy, coupled with expectancy. Faith is activated when you expect the win to become evident in the natural realm.

Find God's favor and friendship. Imagine turning the pages of your life story and finding favor upon favor. Jesus says, "You're living Chapter 26. But take a look at Chapter 31 where My favor pursues you like a hound on a high-speed fox hunt." In the chapters coming up, the story will unfold. But don't wait till Chapter 31 for the good stuff! Be confident of God's friendship. Trust that His favor is pursuing and overtaking you *right now.*

How do you find favor? Favor finds you—but you have to be willing to look around. Actively narrow your focus to zero in on God's goodness. Make what I call "Holy Spirit sweeps." When you step into a crowded room, shift your mind into neutral, look across the room and pray, "Holy Spirit, I'm making a sweep. What are You up to? Who would You like me to engage with? What's the next step?" He will often highlight an individual or group. Be proactive and intentional with your encouragement.

Relax with the Holy Spirit and trust that He's with you in the pain. *"The LORD is near to the brokenhearted and saves the crushed in spirit"* (Psalm 34:18 ESV). There may be days when you're hard on yourself and self-directed bitterness seems to take the upper hand. But remember: your Comforter and Counselor sees every tear and every nightmare. He

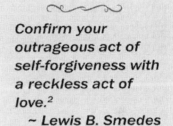

Confirm your outrageous act of self-forgiveness with a reckless act of love.[2]

~ Lewis B. Smedes

knows you. He climbs inside your pain, curls up with you, and holds you close. You belong to Him.

Friend, in your circumstances, what does a win look like as defined by the Holy Spirit?

Core Truth: The object of the game is to live tomorrow's victory today with absolute faith that we'll overcome.

Let's Pray

"Thanks be to God! He gives me the victory through our Lord Jesus Christ" (1 Corinthians 15:57). Father God, I am more than a conqueror through You who loved me. On days when I am tempted to go into victim mode—frustrated, tired, and cross—I declare that I'm an overcomer through You.

I pull future wins into today! Your favor precedes and follows me. I'm making "sweeps" for favor right now. I trust that You're in today's chaos, working for my good, because I've been called according to Your purpose.

Take the Next Step

Sketch a game you like to play. What's the object of the game? On the left side of a page, draw a picture of defeat. Now imagine a sudden overturn. On the right side of the page, draw your win. Label the left side of the page with one word or phrase for a defeated mindset and the right side with that of an overcomer. Who or what shifted things in your favor?

[1]*New Spirit-Filled Life Bible.* Thomas Nelson. 2002. p. 1474.

[2]Lewis Smedes. *Forgive & Forget: Healing the Hurts We Don't Deserve.* HarperCollins. 1996. p. 77.

Section Seven

Community:
Foster Forgiveness

Get Back at the Adversary: Tell Your Story

O God, from my youth you have taught me,
and I still proclaim your wondrous deeds. So
even to old age and gray hairs, O God, do
not forsake me, until I proclaim your might
to another generation, your power to all
those to come.

Psalm 71:17–18 (ESV)

One morning at an elementary school where I taught, I rushed around the production room, preparing paperwork for class. The rumble of buses on the driveway out front announced the kids' arrival. I shoved my hair out of my eyes. I would have just enough time to cut construction paper, but only if I flew.

I grabbed a few sheets of green paper and slid them onto a cutting board. I leaned forward with my school ID tag dangling a few inches above the board and lifted the long-handled blade. I brought it down in one quick motion. *Whack!* I chopped off the lanyard.

What if we could take our regrets and acts of self-directed anger and slash them off with one swift stroke like that?

Sweet Revenge in Story Form

Don't you wish you could avenge every evil act the enemy has done to your camp? You can execute one enormous act of retribution against him: tell your story. When you recount the experiences of God's power, you charge the atmosphere with contagious faith. You engage the power of your testimony.

> **What has God delivered you from? Tell your story and release His redemption. What has God delivered you into? Transform lives with hope.**

"And they overcame him by the blood of the Lamb, and by the word of their testimony" (Revelation 12:11 KJV). When we trust in Jesus, we have the confidence to enter the Most Holy Place by His blood (see Hebrews 10:19).

Christ's redemptive act of dying on the cross brought us forgiveness. No matter what we've done, it's covered by the blood of Jesus. His blood cleanses us and brings us life and hope.

For years, I wanted to hide the anger I leveled at myself. Who'd want to hang around with someone like me? A lot of days, *I* didn't want to hang around with me.

Jesus spoke to my heart: "What if you write your story and describe your journey about forgiving yourself? See the lies in your head? Show others how you've lopped them off, so they can gain freedom."

"Okay, Lord," I agreed. "I'm in."

As I worked and reworked the book in your hands, I hit mental roadblocks. I set it aside for months at a time. I needed to get away to work on the manuscript without interruption. So Emily and I stayed at a beach house on the Washington coast for a week.

Once there, we talked and strolled across the sand. In the quiet spaces in between talks with Emmy, I quieted my heart and asked Jesus, "Lord, why I am having such a hard time writing my book?"

"You call it your book. But it's not *your* story. It's *Mine*. I'll tell the story. You write it down."

Back at the cottage an hour later, I sat down at my laptop computer and asked, "Okay, Lord, what *is* Your story? What do *You* want to say?" The words poured onto the page.

Tell *His* Story

So maybe it's time to tell your story. But you don't need to worry about the words. They'll come from your heart. Besides, it's not *your* story. It's *Jesus'* story in *you*.

The idea of telling people your history might feel a bit intimidating, but transparency opens the door for others to do the same. When I told people how hard it had been to forgive myself, Jesus peeled layers of shame off my soul. The isolation of thinking, "I'm the only one" dissolved.

Testimonies of God's power and healing shift the atmosphere in our circles of influence—prayer gatherings, businesses, ministries, schools, and neighborhoods—and make our interactions more authentic.

Sharing your story can be cleansing. It can serve as part of your healing process. It gives you a chance to be real and to get in touch with your emotions. It allows God to meet you there and to validate you. Then you can release that healing to others so that they can grow.

You may be thinking, "What if my story is 'way out there'? What if no one understands?" Hey, maybe no one has walked a mile in your shoes or even the short trip from your front door to your mailbox, for that matter. But opening your heart, no matter how many twists and turns your past holds, will draw others' attention to how God was glorified. It's not about how you look in the grand scheme of things. It's about lifting Jesus up and *"ascribing to the Lord the glory due His name"* (Psalm 29:2).

A Double Share of Honor

"Instead of shame and dishonor, you will enjoy a double share of honor. You will possess a double portion of prosperity in your land, and everlasting joy will be yours" (Isaiah 61:7 NLT). When we take a step of obedience, we gain a double share of honor because His Spirit lives in us. We can expect Father God to peel off layers of guilt and condemnation, releasing joy in their place.

Do you have to be 100 percent healed to share what He's done so far? No. In church classes I taught, little children got excited about sharing Jesus with their friends. An eight-year-old boy exclaimed, "I get it! I don't have to tell my friends the whole Bible. I just tell 'em what I know."

There you go. Tell 'em what you know. Then expect the supernatural to show up and rise![1]

Core Truth: We avenge the enemy's tactics when we tell our stories.

Let's Pray

Jesus, Lamb of God, I'm overcoming the enemy by Your blood and the word of my testimony. I'm going to exact one enormous act of retribution against the devil. You redeem everything. *Everything.* I'm taking back the years the locusts have eaten—with interest (Joel 2:25). Let's do it. Let's tell *Your* story in me.

Take the Next Step

Write out your story of explosive redemption. Share it with someone this week. If the Holy Spirit prompts you to share it with a larger group, ask Him to guide your next steps.

---

[1] I invite you to share your story at www.lynnhare.com.

Self-Forgiveness as a Lifestyle

But be doers of the word, and not hearers only.

James 1:22 (NKJV)

I love to dance. I might not be the most fluent or graceful in the world, but I love getting swept up in the pulse of the music, swaying and twirling. I enjoy the rush of becoming one with a song—moving, tumbling, and soaring along.

The walk of self-forgiveness has its own cadence—a certain rhythm: walk, sync up with the Holy Spirit, and take a few steps with Him. Walk, sync, and take a few steps more. *"But I say, walk by the Spirit, and you will not carry out the desire of the flesh"* (Galatians 5:16 NASB). When we connect with Him throughout the day, our fleshly tendency to come down on ourselves with negativity dissolves, and we think His thoughts, filled with excitement for possibilities.

Alignment with the Holy Spirit opens our eyes to the truth that self-forgiveness is not a one-time choice or even a series of isolated events. Instead, it's an ongoing attitude and approach to life.

Consider these keys to making self-forgiveness a lifestyle.

Focus on the Holy Spirit's presence. When you fall, don't focus on the hard floor beneath you. Remember that you are covered by grace. Focus on the Holy Spirit Himself. Incredibly, He transforms any situation into a place of godly union.

Remember God's past faithfulness. As you reflect on how He's come through for you in the past, trust that He'll speak to you again in His time. We sometimes need to trust more deeply that God will redeem our errors. We activate that shift when we frame those events in the context of His faithfulness. *"Once God has spoken; Twice I have heard this: That power belongs to God"* (Psalm 62:11 NASB). When we visit and revisit His miracles, we frame our situations with expectation that His power is about to be unleashed again.

Celebrate the face plant. You took a risk. You extended yourself beyond the familiar and explored possibilities. You put yourself out there. Way to go!

We are called to agree with God as he shows us His truth. *"To this end we always pray for you, that our God may make you worthy of his calling and may fulfill every resolve for good and every work of faith by his power"* (2 Thessalonians 1:11 ESV). We resolve to work out our faith with the best of intentions, but setbacks happen along the way. When we demonstrate willingness to take a risk—to be stretched, to be expanded—we take small but meaningful steps.

"Do not despise these small beginnings, for the LORD rejoices to see the work begin" (Zechariah 4:10 NLT). We take a few steps. We falter. We fall. We get back up. Our willingness to get back in the game is an act of worship itself.

It demonstrates our surrender to the process.

He pursues us in love, reaching out to be seen, heard, and sensed—in the middle of our chaos, during the mundane routines of life, and while we celebrate our greatest joys. When we respond and draw near to Him, He communes with us to restore us body, soul, and spirit.

Speak to yourself with compassion, as Jesus does. *"And I will ask the Father, and he will give you another advocate to help you and be with you forever"* (John 14:16). On days when you're heavy-hearted, the Holy Spirit loves to settle in with you. That's when the Comforter and Counselor's touch reaches you deep within. The times you spend in tears are tender, because He shares your grief. What grieves you grieves the Holy Spirit.

Keep short accounts with yourself. Admit, "I blew it! But that's okay, Lord. You love me regardless of whether I get it right. I'm in You. You're in me. Where You go, I go. Your grace is mine."

Put a sticky note on your favorite mirror that says, "And I loved you on that day!" Remind yourself that even on the most terrible days, no matter how badly you might have missed God-truths, His love was, and is, with you. *"And above all these put on love, which binds everything together in perfect harmony"* (Colossians 3:14 ESV).

Ask Jesus for images of restoration. Record your dreams. Write out or draw what you remember. What is He saying to you through them?

Model self-forgiveness for friends and coworkers. When they lash out at themselves, give them grace and remind them that they're accepted. Speak kindly to them.

Expect the Lord to use you to bless others as you make gains in self-acceptance. He might call your attention to specific themes so that you can contend in battle for others. "Maybe I'm off my game," you might reason, "but I can help them. Lord, show me who to pray for!"

"And pray in the Spirit on all occasions with all kinds of prayers and requests. With this in mind, be alert and always keep on praying for all the Lord's people" (Ephesians 6:18). What if this warfare isn't about you after all? Ask the Holy Spirit to lead as you pray for others. What might seem to be a random thought could be just the thing others need from us! I can't count the number of times friends have called, emailed, or texted me out of the blue, and my response was, "I was feeling so discouraged. Your message came at just the right time! Thank you!"

Every time you pray for others, prepare to be amazed. When you set out to comfort and uplift people, expect Christ's strength and healing to flow through you—like electrons flowing through an extension cord as it connects the power source to its destination. Regardless of the prayer flow's target destination, when you pray, you get a piece of the action! *"Those who refresh others will themselves be refreshed"* (Proverbs 11:25 NLT).

Looking Forward to a Better Day

One year, I taught a fun, energetic kindergarten class. Every morning, a five-year-old I'll call Whitney twirled her way down the hallway as we walked to the cafeteria. Secretly, I wanted to encourage her, because her joy made us all grin. But where Whitney's gyrations went, the other children's arms, legs, and bobbing heads followed.

One morning I said, stifling a laugh, "Whitney, I'm sorry, but you can't dance in the hall anymore."

Crestfallen, she asked with moist brown eyes, "When *can* I dance?"

I paused and shot up a prayer. "On the last day of school."

Whitney visibly brightened. "Okay, Mrs. Hare," she grinned. "On the last day, I will dance!"

I laughed softly. When the last day of school came, she'd be dancing up a storm, all right. That reminds me of heaven—and the forever Savior-glory waiting for us. On the last day, we'll dance! After all, He'll wipe every tear from our eyes, and there will be no more death or mourning or crying.

But we don't have to wait until then. Jesus is on the dance floor *now*. When we practice self-forgiveness as a lifestyle, we move with Jesus, as gracefully—or awkwardly—as it goes. No matter how nasty life's days are, Christ's rhythm and grace pulse in us, sweeping us along. Even when we don't know the next move or have all the answers, we can beckon others onto the floor to have a go at their own musical Christ-encounter.

> *What song is Christ singing over you? What dance is He inviting you into?*

Core Truth: Self-forgiveness is not an event. It's a lifestyle.

Let's Pray

Father, I purpose to live a lifestyle of self-forgiveness. Thank You for picking me up when I fall. Thank You that, even when I do a face plant, you celebrate my risks! I purpose to speak to myself with compassion. I'm keeping short accounts with myself. Lord, give me dreams at night that reveal Your heart for me. I purpose to model self-forgiveness to others and bless them in the process.

Take the Next Step

Trace three keys onto a journal page. Label each one with a specific truth to make self-forgiveness a lifestyle. For each one, write a short application statement for your own life.

A Culture of Self-Forgiveness
and Acceptance

*May our Lord Jesus Christ himself and God
our Father, who loved us and by his grace
gave us eternal encouragement and good
hope, encourage your hearts and strengthen
you in every good deed and word.*

2 Thessalonians 2:16–17

I love the pulse of the book that lives and breathes inside
each of us. We scroll through unique adventures, some
more likable than others. Hairpin turns take us off-road.

As we move forward on our spiritual journey, a unique
and wonderful process takes form and shape. We find that
the adventures that took us far from the path where we began
have purpose. Maybe, just maybe, they begin to make sense.
Or maybe parts of the story still don't add up.

Multiplying Grace Like Loaves and Fishes

As we turn one page after another in our book of life, a series
of events unfolds and a theme develops. We no longer attach

our growth to inward-focused thoughts. Each chapter begins with an experience and ends with a plot twist of super-reliance on the Holy Spirit.

The Spirit of the Living God will always direct us to pour out to others. What if the process of self-directed grace is actually about creating a culture of self-forgiveness? Our Heavenly Father desires for us to build a community of forgivers.

Maturity in the Kingdom is about lifting our eyes and hearts to foster others' gain.

"We have different gifts, according to the grace given to each of us. If your gift is prophesying, then prophesy in accordance with your faith; if it is serving, then serve; if it is teaching, then teach; if it is to encourage, then give encouragement; if it is giving, then give generously; if it is to lead, do it diligently; if it is to show mercy, do it cheerfully" (Romans 12:6–8). What is your gift? God has given it to you so that you can give it away.

As I grew, I lifted my spiritual eyes and shifted my focus off myself. I recognized that it wasn't all about me. I asked God to show me how to build up and encourage others.

As I wrote this book, I had you in mind, friend. I purposed to find ways to empower you to forgive, and as I prayed, I asked Jesus if He'd multiply the blessing. When he blessed two fish and five loaves of bread, He released a spirit of multiplication and fed 5,000 people. I pray that the same multiplication through you will empower every life you touch—and beyond.

The Wisdom of Ants

"For the foolishness of God is wiser than human wisdom, and the weakness of God is stronger than human strength" (1 Corinthians 1:25).

Ants are known around the world for their intelligence. They work together to farm and gather food. Some ants serve as soldiers, protecting their colonies. Others are architects, nurses, and construction workers. As a unit, they make decisions together, like choosing the site for a new nest.

Ants are very strong. They can carry a hundred times their body weight. Some build tunnels thousands of miles long. They make assembly lines, highways, and even underground cities. But scientists agree that ants don't demonstrate intelligence on their own. Ants build, collect, and communicate effectively only as a colony.

In the same way, God has created us to work together in community. We plan, build, overcome obstacles, and grow together.

Individually, independent of God and one another, we cannot release the grace of a brilliant Redeemer as effectively as we can as a corporate Body. Corporate wisdom and strength expressed in unity honor God.

Reach Forward and Be an Influencer

Trapeze artists practice long hours. Over and over, on a 30-foot-high platform, they practice proper timing and momentum so they can power forward from a swing, release it, and reach for the next. We can do the same as we let go of focusing on ourselves to reach forward for others' success and engagement.

When we make a commitment to encourage others toward a lifestyle of self-acceptance and self-directed grace, we change the atmosphere. We can welcome renewal arising from the infilling of the Spirit. And when we don't accomplish Kingdom assignments with perfectly neat strokes or polished words, we can celebrate the tangible, realized presence of the Holy Spirit right there in the thick of it all.

When we humbly and openly share our faults, an atmosphere of acceptance and grace forms the core of our relationships. When that happens, we create safe places to grow with a culture of authenticity.

> *Knowing the "life story" the way God has planned it for us . . . we gain the character, fortitude, experience, temperament and ability to leverage our experience, and to positively influence someone . . . God's way.*[1]
> ~ Dr. Gordon Bradshaw

As we shift our focus from ourselves to others, let's remember to share our hard-won victories with the next generation. They will become confident and strong when we encourage them to see and experience the Creator, His love, and their identity in Him.

Together, we can then celebrate one another's discovery that there is no force—not even our own foolish actions—that can separate us from the love of God that is in Christ Jesus our Lord.

Core Truth: A culture of self-forgiveness is found in a community that values honor and grace.

Let's Pray

Lord, I purpose to engage with Your greater move in my home, workplace, church Body, school, neighborhood, and every community where You place me. Together, let's create a culture of self-forgiveness. Who can I encourage today? How will forgiveness foster a greater connectedness? Your grace overflows into and out of everything we do.

Take the Next Step

This week, write and send messages to three people, encouraging them on their journey of self-acceptance.

---

[1]Dr. Gordon E. Bradshaw. *I See Thrones! Igniting and Increasing Your Influence in the Seven Mountains of Culture.* Kingdom House Publishing. 2015. p. 94.

Where's the *Real* Action?

First of all, then, I urge that supplications,
prayers, intercessions, and thanksgivings be
made for all people . . . that we may lead a
peaceful and quiet life, godly and dignified
in every way."

1 Timothy 2:1–2 (ESV)

The car accident with Ben lingered in my mind as I prayed for my own healing over the years that followed. Ben picked up the pace, but I was forced to slow down.

For years I had enjoyed 10-kilometer fun runs with Tim. We had enjoyed tossing a Frisbee and flying kites on the Oregon coast. We rented tandem bikes for weekend excursions and played pick-up games of basketball with friends. But now the long-term effects of back, rib, and foot injuries left me with residual arthritis and a mild limp.

At the top of my game for so many years, I was forced into the role of a spectator.

"Why am I on the bench?" I asked God, envying women playing volleyball and going on long hikes together at church retreats. I wished my foot was stronger so I could stomp it. "I want to be where the real action is!"

I was about to find out that His definition of "action" was altogether different than mine.

A Slower Pace Brings New Friends

In medical clinics over the years, I waited with patients and often heard the Lord whisper, "Pray for them." Something quietly stirred in my heart—a confidence that the Healer's power was released in simple prayers of faith.

In doctors' and physical therapists' waiting rooms, no longer on a mad dash through life, I listened as shy folks shared their stories of financial ruin, shattered dreams, broken families, and illnesses that caused excruciating pain. The Holy Spirit showed me how to enter into their pain and release a quiet hope as we gently prayed.

I moved slowly and was rewarded with newfound elderly friends who hobbled along beside me. They demonstrated faith and godly wisdom they'd gained over many seasons. Their crinkled smiles and soft senses of humor endeared them to me. Little by little, the Lord healed my leg and back injuries.

But 10 years later, debilitating cycles of fibromyalgia sidelined me again. Muscle and joint pain, insomnia, headaches, and brain fog often challenged my ability to work and hang out with friends. Determined to do my part, I refused thoughts that I was a victim.

Instead, I asked God to show me how to contend for those around me. "Maybe I'm off my feet again, but I can help others. Lord, show me who to pray for!"

The Holy Spirit led me to specific Scriptures to pray over friends' situations. I was amazed—every time I prayed for others, I felt a surge of strength and healing, too.

Practicing One Kick

Bruce Lee once said, "I fear not the man who has practiced 10,000 kicks once, but I fear the man who has practiced one kick 10,000 times."[1] I was determined to be known for one kick—intercession. I prayed with thousands of people. We stepped into God's presence, quieted ourselves, and listened together. I encouraged them and grew excited when they heard from Him, too.

Jesus knows when circumstances overwhelm us. He listens as we spend time with Him. Practicing His presence brings restorative healing. How? The more time we spend in prayer, the greater His awakening of our senses to His vibrant life within us.

> In the quiet presence of Christ's transforming power His finest miracles emerge.

God is in the process of peeling off the fibromyalgia, a layer at a time. Arthritis, swelling, and bruising in the foot that was crushed in those floorboards years ago still keep me from running 10-kilometer races or playing volleyball at picnics. I haven't ridden a bike in many years. But I've learned a secret.

The Lord desires a heart that holds still long enough to experience Him fully, attentive ears bent toward His compassionate voice, and a soul that comes expectantly into His presence. Soaking in His transforming power and releasing it into the lives of others—that's where the *real* action is.

Core Truth: The *real* action is found as we're transformed by God's presence in prayer, bringing hope to others on their journeys.

Let's Pray

Holy Spirit, who can I step into Your presence with today?

Take the Next Step

Pray with one person today, helping him or her become still enough to hear the Holy Spirit. Share what you experience.

---

[1]http://www.bruceleequotes.org/category/bruce-lee-quotes/ (Retrieved October 7, 2016.)

Epilogue

Sometimes you tell the story. Sometimes the story tells you.

To my great surprise, the passion for prayer birthed out of a divine collision connected me with a huge network of people who were just as crazy about intercession as I was. When we prayed, God showed up with all kinds of surprises.

Nine years after Ben's neurosurgery at Stanford University Hospital, we were astonished to see his intellect outstrip his peers. Ben tested at the 95th percentile in every subject, which qualified him for the Talented and Gifted program. He took advanced courses with other brainiacs who loved to read, write, and create.

He has a beautiful voice and loves to sing in barbershop quartets and choral ensembles. Six foot two Ben loves the stage and delights audiences at local drama troupe productions and church functions.

On his 21st birthday, Ben and his blue-eyed girlfriend, Jill, stepped onto a dock on the Willamette River in Portland. Surrounded by a gaggle of strutting geese, Ben dropped to one knee and proposed to sweet Jill. That September, he stood beneath a burgundy arbor at the front of a church sanctuary in Newberg, Oregon, as his beautiful bride approached down the aisle.

A few minutes later, a slide show with Ben and Jill's photos, accompanied by the song *100 Years*, played on a big screen overhead. The pictures blurred as tears splashed down my chin onto my beaded dress. I watched Ben grow up. A rough-and-tumble suspender-wearing toddler with summer-bleached hair. A preteen nerd with a flat cap, glasses, and a sideways smile. Resonant, booming bass Nathan Detroit in *Guys and Dolls*. A young man at City Hall, picking up a marriage license with his fiancée.

In my front-row seat at the wedding, I drew in a shaky breath. And as I exhaled, an elephant rolled off my chest. The Redeemer did it. He pulled it off. *Happily ever after.*

Is life perfect? No. Ben still has a facial tic that tugs his face to one side. Headaches come and go. But Jill, who is a lifeguard and swim instructor, their son, Logan, and daughter, Paige, don't seem to notice. To them, he's a remarkably fun, loving husband and father. Today, Ben has three associate degrees and works as a successful developer for our software business.

Andy enjoyed Talented and Gifted classes, too. He mastered the French horn, keyboard, guitar, and drums. He earned a bachelor's degree in Japanese and moved to Japan to follow his dream of becoming a translator.

Emily served on leadership teams for Christian college ministries and is in love with Jesus. She enjoys making crafts, painting, and journaling. She is known far and wide as a listener and encourager.

On the pages of my story, the Holy Spirit has turned chaos, confusion, and pain into ever-growing surges of relentless grace. I'm swept up into the irrational acceptance of the greatest Possibilitarian who ever lived.

Epilogue

As I drive forward, I see in my rearview mirror the car accident of years ago—a dot on the side of a hill, receding into the distance.

God's glory is found not only in the forgiveness of God but in the God of forgiveness Himself. It's all about a friendship with our Creator that stretches wide, long, high, and deep.

Will I blow it again? Yep. But God will be in those moments. In the future, a kind and patient Savior who understands is waiting for me.

He's waiting for you, too.

Appendix A
Make Jesus Your Best Friend

Would you like to make Jesus your best friend? Pray this aloud:

God, I align myself with Your ways. Jesus, I believe that You died on the cross for my sins, rose from the grave, and are alive today. I invite You into my heart to be my best friend. I believe and receive Your forgiveness. Thank You for the fresh ability to hear Your voice, see Your face, and sense Your presence. Holy Spirit, open my spirit to all You have for me.

If you just prayed to make Christ your best friend, I'd love to hear from you! I invite you to email me at lynn@lynnhare.com.

Appendix B
Lynn's Daily Prayer

Holy Spirit, I follow You in everything I do. Flow through my thoughts. Illuminate what You see, hear, and sense. My voice is Yours, releasing hope, encouragement, and love where I go. Your calm center is mine.

I cloak myself with humility. I rid myself of pride, rebellion, offense, accusation, condemnation, unforgiveness, and negativity. I will not be overcome with evil. I'm overcoming evil with good.

I choose to actively forgive those who have hurt me. I pray for them to grow in love and wisdom. I actively forgive myself and am at peace with myself today. Jesus, use my circumstances to grow me to be more like You. Father God, on days when it seems like we're at cross purposes, remind me of Your explosive goodness and faithfulness. Deepen my trust in the process.

I put on the full armor of God: the belt of truth, breastplate of righteousness, ready shoes of peace, shield of faith, helmet of salvation, and the sword of the Spirit, which is the Word of God. I pray in the Spirit all the time. I'm alert and always keep on praying for all the saints (Ephesians 6:10–18).

I welcome the angels You've commissioned to protect me as I carry out my Kingdom assignment. I declare that they guard my feet from striking against a stone (Psalm 91). Commander-in-Chief of the Armies of Heaven, I'm listening for Your voice as I partner with Your angel armies in battle. Nothing can separate me from Your love (Romans 8:38).

Nothing can stop *us*.

I declare my mind is filled with wisdom from heaven, which is first pure, then peaceable, gentle, willing to yield, full of mercy and good fruits, without partiality, and without hypocrisy. I'm known as a peacemaker (James 3:17–18 NKJV).

Holy Spirit, fill me. Speak through me. Use me. Grow Your authority-laden fruit in me. Love, joy, peace, patience, kindness, goodness, faithfulness, gentleness, and self-control are growing in me as I become more like You.

I declare that I'm overcoming the enemy by the blood of the Lamb and the word of my testimony (Revelation 12:11). I'm covered by Your blood, Lord Jesus. Who can I share my story with today?

What the enemy means for harm, use for good (Genesis 50:20). Take my faults and failures and turn them into strengths and successes. When I stumble, leadership skills surface as I show others how to press into You.

When things get tough and seem impossible, with You I declare: *All things are possible!*

Appendix C
Scripture Verses
Our Identity in Christ

1. **I am God's child** (John 1:12).
2. **I am Christ's friend** (John 15:15).
3. **I have been justified** (Romans 5:1).
4. **I am assured all things work together for good** (Romans 8:28).
5. **I am confident that God will perfect the work He has begun in me** (Philippians 1:6).
6. **I have not been given a spirit of fear, but of power, love, and a sound mind** (2 Timothy 1:7).
7. **I am born of God, and the evil one cannot harm me** (1 John 5:18).
8. **I am blessed in the heavenly realms with every spiritual blessing** (Ephesians 1:3).
9. **I am holy and blameless** (Ephesians 1:4).
10. **I am given God's glorious grace lavishly and without restriction** (Ephesians 1:7–8).
11. **I am in Christ Jesus, who is wisdom from God** (1 Corinthians 1:30).
12. **I am redeemed** (Titus 2:14).
13. **I am forgiven** (Colossians 1:14).
14. **I have purpose** (Ephesians 3:11).
15. **I have hope** (1 Thessalonians 1:3).
16. **I am sealed with the promised Holy Spirit** (Ephesians 1:13).
17. **I have been chosen, and God desires me to bear fruit** (John 15:5).

18. **I am seated with Christ in the heavenly realms** (Ephesians 2:6).
19. **God expresses His kindness to me** (Ephesians 2:7).
20. **I have Christ, who is my peace** (Ephesians 2:14).
21. **I have access to the Father by the Holy Spirit** (Ephesians 2:18).
22. **I am a dwelling for the Holy Spirit** (Ephesians 2:22).
23. **God's power works through me** (Ephesians 3:7).
24. **I can approach God with freedom and confidence** (Ephesians 3:12).
25. **I know there is a purpose for my sufferings** (Proverbs 19:21).
26. **I can grasp how wide, long, high, and deep Christ's love is** (Ephesians 3:18).
27. **I am completed by God** (Ephesians 3:19).
28. **I have been called** (2 Timothy 1:9).
29. **I can mature spiritually** (Ephesians 4:15).
30. **I can have a new attitude and a new lifestyle** (Ephesians 4:22–23).
31. **I can be kind and compassionate to others** (Ephesians 4:32).
32. **I can forgive others** (Ephesians 4:32).
33. **I understand God's will for me** (Ephesians 5:17).
34. **I give thanks for everything** (Ephesians 5:20).
35. **I am strong in the Lord and in His power** (Ephesians 6:10).
36. **I am not alone** (Hebrews 13:5).
37. **I am prayed for by Jesus Christ** (John 17:20–21).
38. **I am getting my needs met by God** (Philippians 4:19).
39. **I have the mind of Christ** (1 Corinthians 2:16).
40. **I am no longer condemned** (Romans 8:1).

41. **I can do all things through Christ** (Philippians 4:13).
42. **My heart and mind are protected with God's peace** (Philippians 4:7).
43. **I am persevering** (Hebrews 10:35–36).
44. **I am protected** (John 10:28).
45. **I am a new creation** (2 Corinthians 5:17).
46. **I am delivered** (Colossians 1:13).
47. **I am set free** (John 8:32).
48. **I am more than a conqueror** (Romans 8:37).
49. **I am victorious** (1 Corinthians 15:57).
50. **I am being kept firm to the end** (1 Corinthians 1:8).

Appendix D
Recommended Reading

International Forgiveness Institute www.internationalforgiveness.com   Blog, books, resources on forgiveness

HeartMath www.heartmath.com. Blog, books, research and technologies to connect the physical heart's intelligence with science to reduce stress, build resilience, and improve intuition

How to Forgive Ourselves Totally: Begin Again By Breaking Free From Past Mistakes, R.T. Kendall, Charisma House

Redeeming the Time, Chuck Pierce, Charisma House

Awaken the Sleeper: There Is Only One Truth, Nick Castellano, Uhios Publishing

The Whole Soul: Rescripting Your Life for Personal Transformation, Dr. Gayle Rogers, Kingdom House Publishing

8 Keys to Forgiveness, Dr. Robert Enright, W. W. Norton & Company

Freedom Through Forgiveness, Nathan Daniel, Vision Publishing

The Freedom Factor: Finding Peace by Forgiving Others . . . and Yourself, Dr. Bruce Wilkinson and Mark E. Strong, Zeal Books

Self-Talk, Soul Talk: What to Say When You Talk to Yourself, Jennifer Rothschild, Harvest House Publishers

Who Switched Off My Brain: Controlling Toxic Thoughts and Emotions, Dr. Caroline Leaf, Inprov, Ltd.

Switch On Your Brain: The Key to Peak Happiness, Thinking, and Health, Dr. Caroline Leaf, Baker Books

Choosing Forgiveness: Turning From Guilt, Bitterness, and Resentment Toward a Life of Wholeness and Peace, John and Paula Sandford, Charisma House

4 Keys to Hearing God's Voice, Mark and Patti Virkler, Destiny Image Publishers

Forgive & Forget: Healing the Hurts We Don't Deserve, Lewis B. Smedes, HarperCollins Publishers

The Art of Forgiving: When You Need to Forgive and Don't Know How, Lewis B. Smedes, Ballantine Books, Random House Publishing

Total Forgiveness: When Everything In You Wants To Hold a Grudge, Point a Finger and Remember the Pain, God Wants You To Lay It All Aside, R.T. Kendall, Charisma House

Crafted Prayer: The Joy of Always Getting Your Prayers Answered, Graham Cooke, Brilliant Book House

The Art of Thinking Brilliantly (conference CD set), Graham Cooke, Brilliant Book House

The Mind of a Saint, Graham Cooke (conference CD set), Brilliant Book House

The Name Quest: Explore the Names of God to Grow in Faith and Get to Know Him Better, John Avery, Morgan James Publishing

Broken Children, Grown-Up Pain, Paul Hegstrom, Beacon Hill Press of Kansas City

Appendix E
Core Truths

1. Our past does not define us.

2. Mistakes are opportunities to grow in self-acceptance.

3. Tracking our growth by journaling can help us mark the upward path on our journeys of self-forgiveness.

4. Our self-forgiveness journeys will have more impact with creative illustrations.

5. When we exchange the accuser's lies for God-truths, we're empowered.

6. Promises spoken over others are sometimes God's way of speaking to us.

7. Since Jesus paid the price, we don't have to.

8. The Holy Spirit rewires our minds with His thoughts.

9. When we're in step with the Holy Spirit, we speak to ourselves with a renewed soul.

10. Our thoughts can activate and change the course of events.

11. Speaking God-truths out loud changes the atmosphere and attracts positive changes in our circumstances.

12. When we exercise our authority in Christ, we readily defeat the schemes of the enemy.

13. The enemy will show us where we are about to make gains.

14. The courtroom bench belongs only to God the Judge.

15. Praying key Scriptures releases strength for our next steps.

16. Forgiving others gives us freedom to forgive ourselves.

17. We find healing when we come into resonant frequency with the Holy Spirit's sounds.

18. Focusing on Jesus' presence in our memories brings healing.

19. Sometimes Christ heals us apart from words.

20. We can rely on our Savior and His calming assurance.

21. In time and above it, God redeems our past and releases expansive, explosive possibilities.

22. We can repent once and thank Christ 999 times.

23. We recalibrate by taking three steps back and gaining God's point of view.

24. No matter what others call us, God's names for us reveal our strengths and virtues.

25. Asking the Holy Spirit fresh questions deepens our relationship with Him.

26. When we forgive ourselves, we gain expansive freedom.

27. The object of the game is to live tomorrow's victory today with absolute faith that we'll overcome.

28. We avenge the enemy's tactics when we tell our stories.

29. Self-forgiveness is not an event. It's a lifestyle.

30. A culture of self-forgiveness is found in a community that values honor and grace.

31. The *real* action is found as we're transformed by God's presence in prayer, bringing hope to others on their journeys.

Connect with the Author

Share Your Story

What's *your* self-forgiveness story? Share your God-encounters and encourage others on a similar journey. Email Lynn at lynn@lynnhare.com with the subject line "My Journey of Self-Forgiveness."

Get Your Free Copy of *30 1-Minute Prayers*

Sign up at www.lynnhare.com to receive Lynn's blog in weekly emails, and get a free copy of *30 1-Minute Prayers*. Get filled with Holy Spirit joy, peace and wisdom. Frame your thoughts and transform your day!

Book Lynn to Speak for Your Group

Lynn enjoys speaking for groups and events. For more information, visit www.lynnhare.com.

Connect with Lynn

Website and blog: www.lynnhare.com
Email: lynn@lynnhare.com
Facebook: facebook.com/LynnHareAuthor
Twitter: twitter.com/HareLynn
Instagram: instagram.com/lynnrhare
LinkedIn: linkedin.com/in/lynnhare24

About the Author

 Lynn Hare is an award-winning author, speaker, and certified teacher. She writes about discovering purpose in our journeys, releasing Holy Spirit joy, and finding possibilities in the most unlikely places. Her passion is activating the awareness of our identities in Christ and the explosive freedoms found in forgiveness. She has prayed with thousands of people one-on-one and serves on multiple intercessory teams in the Portland, Oregon area.

Lynn has published devotions, articles, and poetry in numerous Christian periodicals and serves on the Oregon Christian Writers leadership team. Her articles have appeared in *Chicken Soup for the Soul*, *The Upper Room*, *The Secret Place*, *Pathways to God*, *LIVE*, *God's Word for Today*, *Now What?*, *The Christian Journal*, *Breakthrough Intercessor*, and the *Christian Communicator*.

Lynn and her husband, Tim, own a software development business. Their marriage is empirical evidence of God's sense of humor—an extroverted writer and musician married to an introverted Einstein who develops software and business analysis. They have three adult children and two precious grandchildren.

Lynn enjoys photography, writing poetry and songs based on Scripture, and hiking trails along Oregon streams.

28240641R00159

Made in the USA
Columbia, SC
09 October 2018